The
Bone Broth
Miracle

The
Bone Broth
Miracle

HOW AN ANCIENT REMEDY CAN IMPROVE HEALTH, FIGHT AGING, AND BOOST BEAUTY

Ariane Resnick, CNC

Skyhorse Publishing

Skyhorse Publishing books may be purchased in bulk at special discounts for sales promotion, corporate gifts, fund-raising, or educational purposes. Special editions can also be created to specifications. For details, contact the Special Sales Department, Skyhorse Publishing, 307 West 36th Street, 11th Floor, New York, NY 10018 or info@skyhorsepublishing.com.

Skyhorse® and Skyhorse Publishing® are registered trademarks of Skyhorse Publishing, Inc.®, a Delaware corporation.

Visit our website at www.skyhorsepublishing.com.

10 9 8 7 6 5 4 3 2

Library of Congress Cataloging-in-Publication Data is available on file.

Cover design by Laura Klynstra
Cover photo credit Allan Penn

Print ISBN: 978-1-63450-702-8
Ebook ISBN: 978-1-63450-703-5

Printed in the United States of America

Table of Contents

Introduction

Food is my favorite topic of conversation. I'll happily spend hours discussing anything from seafood to seaweed, but the food subject closest to my heart is healing foods. I witness them change the lives of my private chef and nutrition clientele on a daily basis, and I changed the course of my own life with them more than once. When I was told by multiple doctors that my chronic illnesses were likely not fully recoverable and that they would require immense quantities of pharmaceuticals that may or may not be effective, I felt I had no choice but to forge my own path to wellness. My modalities were varied, but the role that food played was pivotal during both health crises. I made complete recoveries from them holistically without much professional guidance, and my food choices enabled my return to wellness. Thankfully, my former illnesses have been in my past for multiple years now, but eating for well-being will always remain a strong aspect of my present. I was fortunate to grow up in a home that focused on the consumption of only whole, organic foods, and I believe that they are our best keys to health. The more we are able to return to eating as nature intended, rather than as chemical companies and factories intend for us, the better our chances of being healthy and happy.

Of all the foods I utilize for wellness, bone broth is easily the one that I would call the closest thing humanity has discovered to a panacea. I have used it to aid my clients' recoveries from leaky gut, SIBO, celiac disease damage, Lyme disease, IBS, sports injuries, and much more. Comprised of little beyond bones and water, the amazing results of bone broth belie its inexpensive ingredients and straightforward preparation. When people are sick with even just a cold, soup is what we innately crave; it is easy on the digestion, it's soothing, and when we are too tired to chew, we can still sip on broth. It is no surprise, then, to learn that the health benefits of bone broth are manyfold. It is commonly believed that for as long as humans have been hunting animals for their meat, we have been boiling their bones too. Physicians as far back as Hippocrates espoused its benefits, and nearly every early civilization had its own versions of bone broth.

The current rise in Paleo eating has brought with it the resurgence of bone broth into popular culture, and eaters of nearly every type of diet are taking notice. Diet trends come and go, and the popularity of a Paleolithic-based diet has been repeatedly passed off as a fad. It differs, however, from ideological plans such as veganism or the low-fat movement in one major way: it is based upon our eating history as a species. By returning to our ancestral roots as much as possible, we return to the healing aids that we never should have left behind. Bone broth is not so much a "food trend" as it is a nod to a very simple, curative tool that nearly everyone can benefit from. In this book I will delve into the many ailments that bone broth can aid, and you may find yourself in awe of how varied they are. We understand that kale is good for everything from helping your brain to preventing cancer, yet people have a harder time acknowledging how many different ailments bone broth can work for. It helps alleviate joint pain, tightens sagging skin, strengthens the immune system, restores intestinal integrity, and provides essential nutrients ranging from amino acids to vitamins and minerals. It may not be green, but it is powerfully strong.

The number one question I am asked about in relation to bone broth is, "Are all bones created equal?" so that topic gets plenty of air time in this text. While the bones of any animal species have their benefits, they each have unique traits. Beyond that, the bones of the animal you use for broth are as important as its meat when you eat a steak or a chop. The industry of factory farming yields inflammatory hormone- and antibiotic-filled animal products that should not be a part of any person's general diet, let alone the foods one chooses for wellness. Using GMO-fed factory-farmed animal bones for broth and expecting it to heal you makes about as much sense as juicing pesticide-laden vegetables and expecting the juice to detoxify you. You are what you eat, as the saying goes, and because of that you are also what your food ate. I will discuss the importance of grass-fed, organic, and wild options. The reasons for choosing those range from ethics to essential fatty acid properties and will make it clear to you that sustainable, humanely raised, organically fed animals are by far the best selection.

The process of making bone broth is so simple that one hardly even needs a recipe, but the cooking times generally considered the norm can be daunting; if you aren't used to spending an hour in the kitchen, you probably aren't looking to spend twenty-four there. Thankfully, modern conveniences such as pressure cookers and slow cookers take the onus off of you from watching the proverbial pot boil. To help you realize how easy it is to create your own bone broth, I will review the assorted methods as well as the benefits of each. Rest assured that it isn't nearly as big a deal as you may fear, and it is pretty foolproof. If you can boil water, you can make bone broth. If you can't boil water, you might as well learn how to with some bones in there!

Of course, I am not going to stop at just teaching you how to make broth, because I understand that most people don't want to sip on it and call it a day. Chances are, you will be most likely to use bone broth as a tool for wellness if you can incorporate it into your culinary lexicon. I'll be sharing recipes for assorted soups and stews, from simple blended vegetable and broth combos to healthier versions of the classics. I'm also going to introduce you to a bevy of herbal tonic recipes that will supercharge your wellness at warp speed. Lastly, did I hear someone say brocktail? Yes, you really can retox your detox with broth! Brocktails were staples at restaurants in the days of yore, and plenty of iconoclast restaurants are bringing them back now. Bone broth turns a cocktail into an adventure, so I have some mixology secrets to share that will not only enliven your entertaining, they'll lessen the blow of alcohol on your system by countering it with some nutrition.

By the time you have reached the end of *The Bone Broth Miracle*, I am confident that you will be a believer in what I have long known to be true: simple, whole food recipes are nature's best medicine, can be delightfully easy to make, and can taste incredibly good. I am thrilled to begin my public culinary discussion with the topic of bone broth, and I know that when you close this book, it will be to make a pot of your own.

What Is Bone Broth?

An age-old culinary staple made new again, bone broth is no longer just an ingredient used to make soups and stews, but also an invigorating health drink. The revitalizing health benefits are numerous, but the first step in becoming acquainted with bone broth is knowing the difference between broth and stock. While the two words have colloquially become interchangeable, the original distinction was in the meat to bone ratio. Initially, broth was considered more palatable on its own because it relied on a greater portion of meat in the cooking process, while stock was made from considerably more bones and was mild in flavor. Commercially available stock is generally cooked for much less time than homemade broth is, and has added flavoring and chemicals that make the nutrient value negligible.

The language of broth has many forms, from the French *bouillon* and *consommé* to Italian *brodo*. *Bouillon* and *brodo* are synonymous with one another, representative of the simmered bones, the *mirepoix* medley of vegetables, and water that makes traditional broth. Consommé is distinct in that it is broth that is clarified using egg whites to amass the solids in the broth so that they can be sifted and filtered out.

The broth-stock debate continues across kitchens and amongst chefs globally, but what we recognize as bone broth today begins from a combination of marrow-filled and cartilage-packed bones, mixed vegetables, water, and a splash of vinegar or citrus. These ingredients are often cooked over the course of several days, which infuses minerals, vitamins, and amino acids from gelatin in the bones into the resulting broth. The combination of nourishing elements and the flavor released in the long cooking process makes bone broth not only good for you, but also richly appetizing.

The Global History of Broth

Let food be thy medicine, and medicine be thy food.
—Hippocrates

Soup may very well be the first example of human cuisine. Heatproof containers perfect for boiling water were invented somewhere between five thousand and nine thousand years ago, but it is possible that cooking broth may go back even further. The recent discovery of heatproof pottery in Xianrendong Cave in China suggests that bowls for cooking and eating were used as early as twenty thousand years ago. Conversely, many archaeologists have speculated that pottery was not even needed for preparing meals, as long as a ditch lined with animal skins and fire-heated rocks were available. While what historians know of the gastronomic evolution of modern humans may never lead to a detailed cookbook, it is widely agreed that the leftover broth from boiling meat and bones was a large part of early diets.

Skipping much further down the culinary timeline come the first written examples of broth. The modern-day word for "soup" comes from the Latin root for "soak," or *suppare*. The transition of this word eventually led to the French word *sope* or *soupe*, and was based on the idea of soaking bread in broth. (This is also the root of the English word for *supper*.) It is fitting then that France may be responsible for the very first modern restaurant, which had its origins in broth-based cuisine. Prior the late eighteenth century, the closest concept to what we know today as restaurants were in fact inns that provided board for their guests. In 1765 in Paris, a man by the name of Boulanger is said to have opened a shop to sell a broth made of sheep's feet simmered in white wine. Story has it that the sign over his shop said *Boulanger débite des restaurants divins*, or "Boulanger provides divine sustenance," due to the restorative quality of the broth. Thus the word "restaurant" then evolved from the motto of the shop selling revitalizing broth to the concept it is today.

Broth itself has continued to be a trusted healing remedy across cultures and amongst grandmothers all over the world. In much the same way of some old medicinal remedies—like moldy bread made into a wound healer prior to penicillin, oats used in bathtubs to soothe chickenpox and skin rashes, and peppermint tea to settle the stomach—broth and chicken soup have been the faithful home treatments for cold, flu, and other maladies for generations. In the twelfth century, the Jewish physician Moses Maimonides wrote extensively on the therapeutic qualities of chicken soup. In his work *Medical Responsa*, Maimonides recommended chicken broth to "neutralize body constitution" and also cure asthma and leprosy. While the leprosy claim did not pan out, the key ingredients in chicken broth were ultimately shown to be anti-inflammatory and assist with cold-related respiratory problems in a 2000 study done by the University of Nebraska Medical Center in Omaha.

Broth has continued to be a valued tradition and comforting cure across time and culture. In various forms, healing soup has been ladled into bowls the world over, from the Greek *avgolemono* and Japanese *tonkotsu,* to Jamaican cow foot soup, Korean *seolleongtang*, Danish *hønsekødssuppe*, and matzoh ball soup, or what many people affectionately refer to as "Jewish penicillin." Traditional chicken noodle soup is one of the most recognizable recipes in the world, and the benefits of its broth continue to have an impact. Today, long-cooked broth in many forms, from poultry and beef to pork and fish, are used in nourishing recipes. The next phase of this age-old meal's evolution is as a hearty and revitalizing health drink.

PART 1: HEALTH BENEFITS

Sources of Bone Broth Matter

Before we can discuss the health benefits of bone broth, there is an important contributing factor as to *why* the broth is so healthful and from which all of this information is based: it is organic. Grass-fed beef, pasture-raised pork, organic poultry, and wild-caught fish are the only acceptable choices for cooking bone broth. There are dozens of environmental reasons for choosing organic farming over industrialized farming, but for the purposes of nutrition, the saying no longer goes *you are what you eat*, but rather, *you are what you eat eats*. The long-boil process in cooking bone broth exacerbates pesticides and toxins that end up in your meat from conventional farming. This is an important idea to keep in mind when making healthy choices with all food products, whether in terms of what the cattle in your steak ate over the course of its life or the pesticides that are sprayed on the vegetables that end up in your salad.

Grass-Fed

Animals that have spent their lives eating grains like corn instead of grass are at a severe disadvantage. By being given the wrong kind of food for their digestive systems, cattle end up malnourished and lacking important vitamins and minerals. In the cattle industry, allowing cows to graze and eat the healthy grass that their bodies evolved to consume is very expensive. Farmers must own acres upon acres of pasture to make up for how quickly cattle can eat through grassy fields. For the farming industry, the switch to corn feed was an economic decision, not a health one. While this may work for the cattle industry and lower prices of meat for consumers, it creates unhealthy animals, and in turn, unhealthy humans. Corn is a starchy, rich food that fattens cows up quickly, putting meat on American tables significantly faster to meet our high demand. However, cows are not naturally able to digest corn, which builds up sludge-like material in their stomachs, causes them to bloat, and can put life-threatening strain on their vital organs. In just the same way that juicing non-organic fruits and vegetables filters pesticides directly into your cup, brewing bone broth with the bones of unhealthy and malnourished animals only concentrates the negative aspects of their diet and brings it directly to yours.

Grass-fed beef has 80 percent less total fat, 30 percent less cholesterol, four times more vitamin E, and ten times more vitamin A than grain-fed cattle do. It contains Omega-3 fatty acids, beta-carotene, and vitamin B6. Not only is grass-fed healthier, but it tastes better, too. The meat is leaner and juicier than the greasy and fatty meats of grain-fed beef. By using grass-fed beef bones in your broth, many of the nutrients and positive benefits of a healthy animal will be passed on to your own diet.

Free-Range & Cage-Free vs. Organic & Pasture-Raised

Chicken feet are an amazing source of gelatin, which contributes to making chicken an ideal choice in choosing bones for your broth. Organic, free-range chicken is the best way to reap these health benefits. Here, semantics matter. The terms "free-range" and "cage-free" are popular buzz words, but do not guarantee healthy chickens on their own. Farms that label themselves as free-range or cage-free do not have to be regulated, meaning that consumers are taking them at their word that the chickens are being well treated, see regular sunlight, and are not confined in close quarters with disease-carrying rodents or in small cages inhaling their own fecal dust for hours of their day. "Organic," however, is an entirely different story. Farms that are permitted to be official producers of organic poultry are regularly audited by the government and therefore have to follow strict regulations. In order for poultry to meet the USDA's National Organic Standards, poultry must be fed completely organic feed, which means that there are no GMO (genetically modified) crops or animal byproducts involved, and no exposure to land that has experienced chemical pesticides or fertilizers in the previous three years. The chickens themselves must be cage-free, have access to the outdoors, and must be free of hormones and antibiotics (unless they have been threatened by disease). As a result, using organic chicken bones ensures that your meals and broth will be similarly free of toxins and full of nutrients. "Pasture-raised" poultry is increasingly popular as well. Many farms that use this term ensure that their poultry spends most, if not all, of their lives with access to the outdoors and are sprout-fed rather than grain-fed. Organic and pasture-raised poultry are your safest bet in finding healthy, nutritious bones for your broth.

Wild-Caught

Using healthy, wild-caught fish in fish-based broths is just as important as using organic meats in meat-based broths. In the open sea and fresh water, fish are free to eat and thrive in their natural ecosystems. Both wild and farm-raised have comparable amounts of cholesterol, protein, and magnesium, but wild salmon, for example, has half the fat, less sodium, 32 percent fewer calories, three times less saturated fat, and higher amounts of Omega-3s than farm-raised fish do, as well as more zinc, potassium, iron, calcium, and vitamin C.

Living conditions are a major concern of farm-raised fish. While the fish being raised in offshore aquaculture may be out in the ocean and not in an industrial plant, they are confined within smaller, netted-off areas that prevent the fish from moving about freely. Overcrowding in these close quarters means that fecal matter and toxins swirl amongst the confined fish, leading to detrimental infestations and disease. These fish can sometimes escape and spread infections to wild fish in other ecosystems. As a result, this means that fish are given high doses of antibiotics. Like other industrialized kinds of farming, raising fish this way negatively affects the environment. Offshore aquaculture does not just impact the fish confined within their nets, but also the surrounding area. Since 1980, nearly one-fifth of the world's mangrove trees have been destroyed in the process of building and running shrimp farms in Southeast Asia, in large part because of the pollution it has caused and the space cleared for its facilities.

When considering which meat and fish to eat in your diet and the bones to use when making broth, there are more factors to consider than just flavor potential and availability. Making conscientious choices about where your food products come from is not only healthier for your diet, but little by little, it helps propel the food industry into making the right decisions in their food-processing plants and farming to benefit animals and the environment.

Collagen and Gelatin: The Foundation for Strong Cartilage, Joints, and Bones

There is more to healthy and strong bones than just eating or drinking your daily dose of calcium. Collagen is found almost everywhere in the body, but primarily in bones and connective tissues. Historically, people have boiled down the collagen-rich bones, skin, and tissue of animals for hearty cooking, but also to transform the collagen into gelatin for glue. Collagen and gelatin are crucial factors in maintaining bone, cartilage, joint, and intestinal health, and are far and away the most healthful elements of bone broth.

Collagen is the protein that holds our frames together. With a strong triple-helix molecular structure, collagen is found in fibrous tissues like skin, tendons, joints, and even blood vessels and corneas. Derived from the Greek word *kolla* for glue, it is the primary component of the body's connective tissue and acts as the skeleton's natural adhesive. Collagen makes up nearly 25–35 percent of the body's protein and is imperative for healthy bones, muscles, and skin.

There are at least twenty-eight different types of collagen in the body, and about five that are the most abundant. Type I collagen makes up much of our bones and can be found amply in the skin, organs, tendons, and vascular ligatures. It is a wound healer, as it is abundant in the material that makes up scar tissue. This kind of collagen accounts for 90 percent of the collagen found in the body. Type II contributes to about 50 percent of the cartilage in the body and is also found in the vitreous humor of the eye. This is the protective gel between the lens and the retina. Type III strengthens hollow organs in the body, like the uterus, intestines, and artery walls. Type IV is the basal lamina, or the makings of the lenses in our eyes. Type V makes up the placenta, hair, and the surfaces of cells. It is second in line to Type I as the most common kind of collagen found in the body.

Together, the different types of collagen help build sturdy bodies, strong joints, healthy organs, and beautiful skin. Without it, muscles can weaken, bones become brittle, and skin loses its elasticity—or in other words, becomes wrinkly. As we age, we see the effects of diminishing collagen from the wear and tear in our bones and joints to the sagging bags underneath our eyes.

Gelatin is the source we use to replenish the collagen in our body, and it is made up of about 84–90 percent protein. While collagen is a protein coming directly from the body, gelatin is a food product made by denaturing—or cooking—foods that contain collagen. This process is something that we do regularly when cooking meals but rarely think about it in that way; by roasting, boiling, grilling, braising, or otherwise cooking meat that contains collagen-rich bones, skin, and connective tissue, natural gelatin is being added to our food. In powdered form, it becomes a translucent agent when preparing food, from commonly thought of desserts like Jell-O and gummy bears, to yogurt, pudding, dips, and ice cream. Outside of food, gelatin is also used as a gelling agent in pharmaceuticals, cosmetics, and photography. Its utility in our daily lives is seemingly never ending.

Amino Acids

The benefits of gelatin in food have a lot to do with the amino acids released in its production. Namely, non-essential amino acids like glycine, glutamine, proline, and alanine are present in gelatin and can do wonders for the body. They are called "non-essential" because technically, the body is capable of producing them on its own. However, when the body is stressed, healing injury, or funneling out other toxins, the body may not be able to keep up with the demand. It is important to eat foods rich in collagen so that the body is never deprived of these reparative resources.

Glycine

Glycine is a building block to protein. The smallest of the amino acid structures, glycine is non-essential, meaning that the body can produce it with other existing chemicals in healthy individuals. Even for the healthiest of people, periodic illness, infection, or pregnancy can strain the naturally occurring levels of glycine. For those suffering from chronic ailments like inflammation, the body may not be able to make up the necessary glycine to support the whole body. Maintaining a healthy diet with foods like bone broth that contain collagen can help strengthen the body's supply of glycine.

Glycine participates in the production of muscle tissue and conversion of glucose into energy. It is also found in the skin and connective tissues and makes up nearly one-third of the collagen structure. For its wound-healing properties, glycine has been used in topical creams for skin ulcers and other skin abrasions.

As a glucogenic amino acid, glycine assists in regulating blood sugar levels, energy levels, DNA and RNA, and the production of bile in the stomach in order to digest fats. It is often used as an ingredient in store-bought antacids for this reason and is recommended by doctors to aid in gastrointestinal disorders and acid reflux. It has been used in treating symptoms of hypoglycemia, chronic fatigue syndrome, anemia, and other problems associated with low energy in the body.

Glycine is also useful in the body's detoxification process. The liver is the body's natural filter of toxins—from alcohol, narcotics, and prescription drugs to preservatives, chemicals, and other impurities in the blood coming from the digestive tract. Small amounts of glycine have been shown to provide protective benefits for the liver, particularly in the harmful effects of alcohol.

Glycine is most often found in foods high in protein, like legumes, dairy, fish, and meat products. Incorporating these foods into your diet on a regular basis helps ensure that the body has the strengthening amino acids that it needs to thrive.

Glutamine

Another non-essential amino acid, glutamine or glutamic acid assists the body in gut health and immunity and is primarily made and found in the body's muscles. The blood distributes glutamine throughout the body, directing it to the places that need it most. It stimulates immune cells and is crucial in cell proliferation in muscles, which benefits all sorts of healing processes for ailments in the body like burns, trauma, injuries, illnesses, stress, and even the healing and regrowth of villi in the small intestines. Intestinal villi are small strands that project from the intestinal wall that make it easier for the intestines to absorb nutrients during digestion. For individuals whose villi have been compromised by gut disorders like Crohn's disease, celiac sprue, and ulcers, the restorative power of glutamine is even more important.

Glutamine can also be helpful for weight problems, both in terms of excessive weight and underweight. Doctors and nutritionists have always recommended nutrient-rich soups as a part of a healthier diet and for calorie control, but the glutamine in the broth is restorative for muscle proteins and helps prevent atrophy, which is when the muscles deteriorate due to malnourishment or lack of use. Atrophy occurs when the body is overworked and is using up more glutamine than muscles can reasonably replenish. Alternatively, the glutamine in soups helps curb cravings for carbohydrates and sugar, which are arguably the two most problematic food addictions for Americans. This boost in metabolism helps maintain healthy muscles and is an essential part of the nourishing enhancements of bone broth.

A Note on Free Glutamates and MSG

Just as many people are sensitive to MSG (monosodium glutamate), it is also possible to be sensitive to natural glutamine. MSG is a synthetic food additive that stabilizes natural glutamate with sodium. The result is a powerful flavor enhancer referred to as "umami" that we often associate with Chinese-American food. The reality is that MSG can appear in many other kinds of processed foods and cause uncomfortable side effects like headaches, inflammation and swelling, heart palpitations, sweating, and nausea. While natural bone broth does *not* contain MSG, free glutamates are released in the long boil process and can affect those who are extra sensitive. Bone broth recipes typically call for the addition of vinegar, which helps release all of the bone's healthy minerals and amino acids—including glutamine. If you are especially sensitive to free glutamates, the addition of vinegar may aggravate this problem. This is most common in those who have chronic illnesses, and does not tend to occur in well people.

Proline

Proline is a fundamental part of collagen and cartilage production. It is prevalent in animal protein, and therefore it is unlikely that individuals who consume healthy, omnivorous diets will ever suffer from insufficient amounts of proline. For many Americans, however, high-carbohydrate, low-fat, and low-protein diets are the norm, which can become problematic for proline production and maintaining healthy skin and connective tissue.

Alanine

Alanine supports liver function, glucose production, and the citric acid cycle, which merges fat, protein, and carbohydrate production. This non-essential amino acid is the supplement of choice for many athletes. While the body makes alanine independently, additional doses of it create the potential to build greater muscle mass and increase endurance. While many people associate this supplement with body builders, it can also be beneficial to the elderly who have weakened muscles and strained physical movement.

These four amino acids that act as the main components of collagen are the vital resources that bodies in times of stress so desperately need. While they are non-essential amino acids, this does not mean there is an everlasting supply. Glutamic acid (glutamine), proline, glycine, and alanine are the four most prevalent amino acids in collagen, and their nourishing effects can be added to anyone's diets simply by drinking or using bone broth in cooking. Studies have shown that cooking chicken broth for long periods of time tripled glutamine content and quadrupled proline, glycine, and alanine content over broths that were only cooked for a short period of time. Healthy diets filled with animal protein and nourishing vegetables help support the production of these amino acids and the role they play in building and maintaining collagen in the body. In the American diet, more people choose to eat boneless meats like chicken or turkey breast in order to avoid fat and for easier preparation and handling. As a result, the parts of the animal that are dense in collagen are tossed away, as are all of the great benefits of their consumption. Unless this cultural tendency toward only eating muscle meats shifts to include more bone meats, adding bone broth to everyone's regular diet can counteract this problem.

Vitamins and Minerals in Bone Broth

Among the many health benefits of bone broth is the mineral content of this slow-cooked nourishing liquid. Minerals like calcium, magnesium, phosphorous, and potassium are released over the course of several hours as the bone softens and breaks down in the simmering heat. While the precise amount of these minerals in each batch of broth can differ depending on how long the broth is cooked for, whether the bones are organic and grass-fed or not, how healthy the animal was, and other mitigating factors, the estimated mineral content in broth is a welcome addition to an already healthy practice of consuming broth regularly in your diet.

Calcium

Calcium is one of the most important minerals that we as humans require to thrive. As a part of a healthy diet, calcium is regularly needed in combination with vitamin D in order to keep bones dense and strong throughout one's life. Vitamin D helps absorb calcium into the body, which is why many milk and juice products reference vitamin D along with calcium on their packaging. Particularly later in life, bones tend to get brittle, break down, and are vulnerable to breakage and fractures. Ninety-nine percent of the calcium in the human body is found in bones and teeth, which means that it is all the more important to maintain calcium levels and take care of our skeletons as we age.

In addition to brittle bones, lack of calcium over the long term can lead to such unpleasant and life-threatening health ailments as blood clotting and rickets, which is an early childhood disease often found in developing countries that can cause deformities in children's skeletal growth.

Calcium is required to help prevent osteoporosis, which can affect both men and women, but is particularly common in menopausal women. Osteoporosis means "porous bones," and is a progressive bone disease that affects bone mineral density. With the rapid decrease in bone mass and density as women age and hit menopause without proper calcium supplementation, the risks of osteoporosis are much greater, and any slip or fall can lead to more severe consequences than in women with healthier bone structures. The most common areas for breakage in women with osteoporosis are the hips, wrists, ribs, and spine.

Osteoporosis can occur more commonly based on heredity, stature (smaller frames being more prone to risk), prior history of fractures, vitamin D deficiency, tobacco use, inactivity, and potentially even the over-consumption of soft drinks.

Doctors recommend increasing levels of calcium over the course of a lifetime, though it is not recommended to consume calcium in excess either. According to the National Institute of Health, the table below indicates the recommended daily doses of calcium for each male and female age group, whether consumed through food, beverages, or dietary supplements:

Age Group	Women Per Day	Men Per Day
Infants 0–6 months	200mg	200mg
Infants 7–12 months	260mg	260mg
Toddlers 1–3 years	700mg	700mg
Children 4–8 years	1,000mg	1,000mg
Children 9–13 years	1,300mg	1,300mg
Adolescents 14–18 years	1,300mg	1,300mg
Adults 19–50 years	1,000mg	1,000mg
Adults 51–70 years	1,200mg	1,000mg
Adults 71+ years	1,200mg	1,200mg

Chewable supplements available in vitamin stores and pharmacies can cover the entire daily dose of calcium, but are not as bio-available (absorbable by the blood). No one serving of food will cover this amount, which is why it is important to have well-rounded, vitamin-rich meals throughout the day. Keep in mind that vegetables have better bio-availability than dairy products, and fortification in dairy products does not lead to bio-availability of nutrients and can often work against it. The best food sources of calcium are dairy products like cow's milk and yogurt. Eight ounces of plain yogurt can make up to 42 percent of an adult's daily intake of calcium. Grains do not typically contain a lot of calcium, but calcium-fortified grains can contain 100 percent of the daily dose.

For many people, dairy and grains aggravate health issues or go against ethical choices in their food. In these instances, calcium-rich vegetables like kale, collard

greens, radishes, turnip greens, and broccoli; seaweeds like kelp; and nuts like almonds and hazelnuts are great options. Compared to yogurt, these have far fewer doses of calcium, but when combined over the course of the day can satisfy the overall levels. Below is a list of serving sizes and daily percentage values of calcium of some of the above food products based on the 1,000mg recommended dose.

Food	Serving Size	Calcium Level	%DV
Plain yogurt	8 ounces	415mg	42%
Nonfat milk	8 ounces	299mg	30%
Raw kale	1 cup	100mg	10%
Turnip greens	½ cup	99mg	10%
Raw broccoli	½ cup	21mg	2%

In one 1934 study at King's College Hospital of London, calcium levels in bone broth constituted 12.30–67.7mg per cup, which falls between 1 and 7 percent of the recommended daily dose of calcium. In contrast, store-bought cans and cartons of broth are labeled as having less than 1 percent the daily amount of calcium, come from grain-fed and factory-farmed animals, and contain loads of preservatives.

To get the most calcium out of your bone broth, the combination of at least one cup of broth and many calcium-rich vegetables will play a part in fulfilling the recommended daily dose of this very important vitamin. Hearty soups made from ingredients like bone broth, kale, turnips, and kelp noodles can be a delicious way to achieve this goal.

Magnesium

The average adult body contains roughly 25 grams of magnesium. Of this amount, 50–60 percent can be found in the bones, playing an active role in the structural integrity of the bone. This important mineral contributes to three hundred enzyme systems throughout the body, affecting energy production, blood glucose control, nerve impulses and muscle function, protein synthesis, and more. Magnesium also takes part in the synthesis of DNA, RNA, and processes that help the regulation of blood pressure and heart rhythm. The kidneys reliably maintain much of the body's magnesium production in healthy individuals, but poor diet, chronic alcoholism, and certain medications can lower these levels. Regular additions of magnesium-dense foods in an individual's food regimen can counteract these low levels, as the body is able to absorb approximately 30–40 percent of all diet-related magnesium.

Without the proper amounts of magnesium, health conditions like magnesium deficiency and hypomagnesaemia can occur. The symptoms of magnesium deficiency can include muscular problems like spasms, tremors, cramps, and weakness; nausea and vomiting, fatigue, loss of appetite, and memory problems. Other symptoms can include rapid heartbeat, retention of sodium, low calcium and potassium levels, and, in the most extreme cases, heart failure. While these do not always occur, an estimated 57 percent of Americans do not get the recommended daily dose of magnesium through the dietary choices they make.

Hypomagnesaemia, while similar to magnesium deficiency in signs and symptoms, is an electrolyte imbalance that causes low magnesium levels in the blood. Having one does not necessarily indicate that the other ailment is present, however. Hypomagnesaemia occurs when there are low levels of magnesium that are the result of a systemic problem, rather than magnesium deficiency, which tends to occur as a result of poor health and diet.

Sources of magnesium can be found in vegetables and meat, beverages, water, fortified grains, and dietary supplements. According to the National Institute of Health, the table below indicates the appropriate daily doses of magnesium for each male and female age group, whether consumed through food, beverages, or dietary supplements:

Age Group	Women Per Day	Men Per Day
Infants 0–6 months	30mg	30mg
Infants 7–12 months	75mg	75mg
Toddlers 1–3 years	80mg	80mg
Children 4–8 years	130mg	130mg
Children 9–13 years	240mg	240mg
Adolescents 14–18 years	360mg	410mg
Adults 19–30 years	310mg	400mg

| Adults 31–50 years | 320mg | 420mg |
| Adults 51+ years | 320mg | 420mg |

Dietary supplements, particularly ones absorbed in water, are an easy way to meet the recommended daily dose of magnesium. On the other hand, there are many delicious foods that can accommodate healthy amounts of magnesium, like leafy green vegetables, legumes, nuts, fish, and meat. Some examples of these foods are dry roasted almonds, steamed spinach, black beans, peanut butter, avocado, brown rice, Atlantic salmon, halibut, chicken breast, or ground beef. These are just a few among many healthy foods that contain high levels of magnesium, and below is a list of serving sizes and daily percentage values of magnesium based on the 400mg recommended dose.

Food	Serving Size	Magnesium Level	%DV
Roasted Almonds	1 ounce	80mg	20%
Steamed Spinach	½ cup	78mg	20%
Avocado	1 cup	44mg	11%
Brown Rice	½ cup	42mg	11%
Atlantic Salmon	3 ounces	26mg	7%
Raisins	½ cup	23mg	6%

Dietary surveys in the United States have unfailingly shown that the majority of the populace does not get enough dietary magnesium. While this can be altered by the consumption of magnesium supplements and multivitamins, the reality is that these mineral insufficiencies have a lot to do with the collective population's poor food choices and low standards for the commercial food industry. Hearty bone broth, paired with organic food sources that are brimming with magnesium as listed above, can help improve individual health and avoid painful side effects related to low magnesium levels.

Potassium

Potassium, like calcium and phosphorous, is one of the body's most prevalent minerals. The body uses potassium to maintain a balance in bodily fluids, keep blood pressure steady, help muscles contract, and lower the risks of bone loss and the development of kidney stones. For healthy individuals, the kidneys help regulate potassium levels. Healthy levels of potassium can also help prevent stroke and hypertension.

When levels of potassium get dangerously low in the body, heart rate can increase and cause hypertension, otherwise known as high blood pressure. Hypertension can develop over the course of many years, and is evident when comparing the rate at which the heart pumps blood to how narrow the artery walls are. When left unchecked, high blood pressure can lead to severe health risks like stroke and heart attack.

Sources of potassium can be found abundantly in many fruits, vegetables, milk products, and dietary supplements. The table below indicates the suggested daily doses of potassium over the course of a lifetime for both men and women, whether consumed through food, beverages, or dietary supplements:

Age Group	Recommended Dose Per Day
Infants and Toddlers 1–3 years	3,000mg
Children 4–8 years	3,800mg
Children 9–13 years	4,500mg
Children and Adults 14+ years	4,700mg

There are many healthy foods that are incredibly high in potassium content. Spinach, leafy greens, sweet potatoes, dried apricots, nuts like almonds and pistachios, bananas, coconut water, avocados, broccoli, tomato, cantaloupe, plain yogurt, and strawberries are just a few. The chart below shows examples of serving sizes and daily percentage values of potassium in some of these delicious foods based on a 3,500mg daily value.

Food	Serving Size	Potassium Level	%DV
Swiss Chard	1 cup	961mg	27%
Acorn Squash	1 cup	896mg	26%
Steamed Spinach	1 cup	840mg	24%
Banana	1 cup	540mg	15%

| Tomato | 1 cup | 430mg | 12% |
| Strawberries | 1 cup | 255mg | 7% |

With a balanced and healthy diet, it is exceptionally easy to fulfill the recommended intake of potassium and benefit from its nourishing, heart-healthy effects. Drinking a cup of mineral-rich bone broth every day can help meet these levels, and even more so when added to soups and stews with other vegetables high in potassium.

Phosphorous

Phosphorous is most often found in the teeth and bones, acting as a vital mineral in their structural growth and repair. It is also a chief contributor to successful nerve and muscle function, kidney function, and maintaining a normal heartbeat. Phosphorus can be found in every cell of the human body, and as such, it is no surprise that it adds up to 1 percent of an individual's total body weight. This key mineral helps regulate the use of fats and carbohydrates, as well as assist the growth and repair of cell tissue through protein production.

In individuals who maintain a healthy, well-rounded diet, phosphorous deficiency is very unlikely. However, in much the same way that calcium is stressed as a vital mineral that helps maintain strong bones, so too is phosphorus. The two minerals work together to help keep bones, teeth, and the skeleton as a whole from becoming brittle and prone to breakage over the course of a lifetime. Phosphorus deficiency tends only to happen to individuals with very severe malnutrition; however, staying aware of vitamin and mineral intake to protect the bones and joints is increasingly more important in aging adults. In very extreme cases, the symptoms of phosphorus deficiency can include muscle and neurological dysfunction. Alternatively, *too much* phosphorus can be a hindrance as well, leading to the hardened deposits of phosphorus and calcium in muscles and other soft tissues. Individuals with severe kidney disease and issues regulating calcium will have high levels of phosphorus in the blood.

The table below shows the Institute of Medicine's dietary recommendations for daily phosphorus intake over the course of a lifetime:

Age Group	Recommended Dose Per Day
Infants 0–6 months	100mg
Infants 7–12 months	275mg
Toddlers 1–3 years	460mg
Children 4–8 years	500mg
Children & Adolescents 9–18 years	1,250mg
Adults 19+ years	700mg

Food sources high in protein and calcium are generally considered to be good sources of phosphorus as well. Fruits and vegetables do not contain as much phosphorus, nor do breads and cereals made from refined flour. Even so, the chart below with a few examples of foods high in phosphorus depicts just how quickly the necessary daily content of phosphorus can be reached. The following is based on a 700mg daily value:

Food	Serving Size	Phosphorus Level	%DV
Cooked turkey	1 breast	2183mg	312%
Pumpkin seeds	1 cup	1591mg	227%
Cooked chicken	1 breast w/ skin & bone	1135mg	162%
Whole milk	1 cup	993mg	142%
Split peas	1 cup	632mg	90%
Raw lentils	1 cup	564mg	80%

Phosphorus is truly abundant in most food categories, and the necessary amounts to maintain healthy bones and teeth are easily manageable with access to fresh food products. Only in cases of severe malnutrition is the lack of phosphorus a true problem, but the relationship between phosphorus and calcium—which is not always as simple to come by in one's diet—is very influential in maintaining the sturdy structure of bones throughout the body. The levels of phosphorus in bone broth, paired with phosphorous-dense foods like turkey, chicken, lentils, and countless other fresh foods, can all more than cover the recommended amounts of the mineral needed to stay healthy. What's more, all of these great ingredients can be found in soup and stew recipes in this book.

Bone broth plays host to several vitamins and minerals that are crucial to sustaining bone, joint, heart, sensory, and overall health. As discussed in this section, minerals like calcium, magnesium, potassium, and phosphorus are all main players in this dynamic. While there is no one naturally occurring superfood that will have 100 percent of the recommended doses of each mineral, bone broth and other thoughtfully selected fresh foods can work together to fulfill these dietary needs. The practice of drinking bone broth every day can help add these minerals to your diet, but having bone broth in the house on a regular basis creates more opportunities to bring other invigorating foods into your routine through preparing soups, stews, tonics, and other meals. By being mindful of all of the vitamins and minerals found in these fresh, organic foods, the exercise of incorporating them into a regular diet will become second nature. Over time, the benefits of having these minerals in your diet will manifest themselves in many different ways, but maintaining strong bone health will be one that will have an effect for years to come.

Conjugated Linoleic Acid (CLA)

CLA is an essential Omega-6 fatty acid that is found in grass-fed meat and dairy products. It regulates cellular activity and has been attributed to weight loss, increased metabolism, muscle growth, lowing of cholesterol and triglycerides, and a bolstered immune system. According to a report in the *American Journal of Clinical Nutrition* in May of 2007, researchers at the University of Wisconsin found that modest weight loss could occur in individuals who took 3.2 grams of CLA supplements per day. To steer away from supplements and provide some perspective on this on a real food level, ground beef from grass-fed cattle offers 4.3mg of CLA per gram of fat. Alternatively, chicken only contains 0.9mg and pork only contains 0.6mg. The consumption of grass-fed beef in a regular diet, from drinking health boosting beef bone broth or preparing soups, stews, and other hearty meals from beef broth, can help bring the benefits of CLA into every individual's diet.

Alpha-Linolenic Acid (ALA)

ALA is an essential Omega-3 fatty acid that is commonly found in seeds, vegetables, nuts, and some red meats. Omega-3s can help to prevent blood clotting, reduce inflammation, and even aid in preventing heart disease and heart attacks. Dietary intake of ALA is significantly more effective than supplementary, and has been shown to reduce heart attacks by 59 percent over the course of several years. One University of Maryland Medical Center study showed that Omega-3s like ALA may help in healing certain inflammatory bowel disorders like Crohn's disease. In some studies, grass-fed lamb was significantly higher in omega-3s— more than 25 percent—than commercially raised lamb, with nearly 50 percent more ALA content. Dietary ALA should translate to roughly 1 percent, or 2 grams, of your daily calorie intake. Introducing grass-fed meats like lamb into your diet or bone broth preparation can help provide the ALA your body needs.

Bone Broth Healing

Inflammatory Disorders

Inflammation, when functioning properly in the body, is a good thing. It is the body's way of responding to dangerous attacks and bringing in resources to fix or rid the body of these hazards. When an individual experiences trauma, physical injury, burns, or even small nuisances like splinters in the skin or dust in the eye, inflammation is the response that makes the area swell, feel hot, get red, and feel painful. The immune system then sends white blood cells to clear out or destroy the problem. Situations like these, when stimuli hurt or damage the body and then inflammation kicks in to repair the affected areas, is called an innate response. It is a generic reaction to foreign agents or stimuli.

As a process of the immune system, inflammation also exercises adaptive immunity. This is when the body is encroached upon by an illness or other pathogens like bacteria, fungi, and other viruses, and the immune system learns what it is, destroys it, and then remembers it the next time it happens. This is why when individuals experience certain illnesses, they can build up immunities and either suffer fewer symptoms the next time, or none at all.

A pitfall of these bodily responses is that sometimes they can become chronic. Oftentimes this has to do with external stressors, like diet and environmental contaminants that are persistently causing inflammation in the body. This is severely detrimental to overall health, not just the affected areas, because it puts the body under constant stress and in perpetual defense mode. Foods that are filled with preservatives, made from processed vegetable oils, sourced from non-organic farms, or otherwise exposed to toxins like chemicals and pesticides can all contribute to chronic inflammation. Considering these triggers, chronic inflammation is often a key symptom of serious illnesses like diabetes, heart disease, stroke, obesity, arthritis and osteoporosis, cystic fibrosis, fibromyalgia, and depression and anxiety.

Symptoms of chronic inflammation can be controlled with medicine, but not cured. The best way to prevent inflammation is to start with a healthy diet comprised of anti-inflammatory foods. By disrupting the causes of inflammation and removing them from the surrounding environment or regular diet, individuals susceptible to inflammation can prevent it from occurring at all. For those who have lived with chronic inflammation due to poor diet, illness, or environmental contaminants, making healthy lifestyle changes can drastically alter and even repair the damage that has been done to the body.

As a soothing home treatment that has been trusted for generations, bone broth has been proven to reduce, repair, and prevent inflammation and its underlying causes. Paired with healthy eating, activity, and awareness of the potential triggers of inflammation, individuals can reduce if not completely rid their lives of these ailments. With daily cups of bone broth or by adding gelled broth to recipes, the positive anti-inflammatory benefits can be an easy, unobtrusive way to regularly prevent these disruptive inflammatory disorders.

Leaky Gut Syndrome

Leaky gut syndrome, while not yet recognized as an official medical condition, is a possible diagnosis proposed in many nutritional circles explaining several long-term and serious illnesses. The gut is the largest immune system organ, which means doctors and researchers are still investigating many of the causes of everyday ailments and serious disorders related to it. Advocates of the leaky gut diagnosis suggest that poor diet, infection, alcoholism, certain medications and antibiotics, and parasites can lead to malfunctioning gateways in the gut, perforations in the gut wall, or otherwise compromises in the integrity of the intestinal lining.

This breakdown of the intestinal wall is called intestinal permeability or hyperpermeability, meaning that the perforations can allow dangerous toxins, microbes, and waste to leak through the intestines and enter the blood stream. NSAIDs, or Nonsteroidal Anti-Inflammatory Drugs, like ibuprofen are meant to decrease inflammation in affected areas, but can sometimes have detrimental consequences in the body. Especially when paired with alcohol, these medications can break down the lining of the gut, thus contributing to leaky gut syndrome.

The possible symptoms of this disorder are food sensitivities and seasonal allergies; skin irritations like acne, eczema, or rosacea; gut irritation like bloating, gas, aches, and even irritable bowel syndrome; and hormonal imbalances like depression and anxiety. More serious reactions have been purported to be auto-immune diseases like lupus, celiac disease, psoriasis, rheumatoid arthritis, and Hashimoto's thyroiditis.

With more research, doctors can better understand the causes of leaky gut syndrome and healthy ways to treat those who are suffering from it. Many of the suspected causes of leaky gut syndrome are concerned with compromised intestinal walls, and as such, healing bone broth can play a major role in taking control of your own healing. The glutamine in bone broth helps protect gut lining, which can hinder the biggest cause of leaky gut syndrome. Not only this, but as a soothing beverage with anti-inflammatory benefits, bone broth can reduce the need for anti-inflammatory medications like ibuprofen that can contribute to these harmful gut perforations.

Celiac Disease

Celiac disease, sometimes known as celiac sprue, is an autoimmune disorder that affects the small intestine. It is caused by a negative reaction to gliadin, a gluten protein that is found in wheat, as well as in some forms of barley and rye. It affects the genetically predisposed and occurs somewhere in between 1 and 100 or 1 and 170 people, depending on the population. When an affected person ingests gliadin, the immune system and the small-bowel tissue attack one another, which causes an inflammatory response. The villi lining of the small intestine then experience what is called villi atrophy, meaning that the villi are damaged and the process of absorbing nutrients is interrupted or halted completely.

This disruption in the bowel makes it difficult or impossible to absorb minerals, nutrients, and fat-soluble vitamins like A, D, E, and K, which can have serious side effects. The symptoms are primarily gastrointestinal, including chronic diarrhea, mouth ulcers, severe abdominal cramping, and bloating. Other more serious side effects include weight loss from the inability to absorb carbohydrates and fat, fatigue, failure to thrive in small children, anemia, and osteoporosis or osteopenia due to a reduced mineral content and weakening in the bone. In some cases, complications of celiac disease can also lead to lactose intolerance. If undiagnosed, sufferers can spend years with chronic pain and discomfort. There is currently no medical treatment or cure for celiac disease other than a change in diet.

A lifelong commitment to healthy foods that do not contain the gluten protein is the only manner in which one can avoid the disease's costly symptoms. The major difference between celiac disease and a wheat allergy or intolerance is that they cause reactions in different parts of the immune system. Celiac sufferers continuing to eat wheat can damage the intestines and contract further autoimmune disorders as a result of the malabsorption of nutrients. Those with wheat allergies, however, will not experience the same damage to the intestines and instead will have reactions like wheezing, swelling, diarrhea, and abdominal pain. Those with wheat *intolerances* are those who experience discomfort while wheat is in the system, but will recover and experience no permanent damage thereafter. Celiac sufferers also tend to have more acute reactions to food products containing trace amounts of the gluten protein, like vanilla extract, whereas those with less severe conditions can often digest them without discomfort or reaction.

While consuming bone broth is not a cure for celiac disease, it is a method of healing the injured intestinal walls of those who suffer from celiac disease. Glutamine is an important amino acid that can rebuild and strengthen the intestinal villi after they have atrophied. These repairs to the villi promote better absorption of the nutrients so desperately needed for people to thrive. Considering that a strict gluten-free diet is not without its hazards—whether a food product is incorrectly labeled and contains gluten or other mistakes in which celiac sufferers consume gluten products—it is necessary to have a holistic way to treat the pain that results. The inflammation caused by celiac in the small intestines can be reduced by drinking soothing bone broth, and this can become a reliable method of repairing damage from fluke contaminations or relapses. Once the inflammation is lessened and the villi are healed, those suffering from celiac can rely on bone broth to continue the path to healthy eating.

Small Intestine Bacterial Overgrowth (SIBO)

Small intestine bacterial overgrowth is a condition in which the normal homeostasis of the bacteria in the small intestines is disrupted. The gastrointestinal tract is a continuous muscular system that works together to push digesting food through the tract all the way to the colon. While it is normal for the small intestines to contain some forms of bacteria, it is typically in much smaller proportions than in the colon, and a different set of bacteria altogether. In cases of SIBO, the muscular function that assists the movement of food through the digestive tract is interrupted or immobilized, which causes the bacteria in the small intestines to multiply to higher levels than is normal. This pause in muscular movement can also cause the bacteria from the colon to move backward into

the small intestine. The abundance of foreign bacteria is toxic to the typically less-bacterial environment of the small intestines.

The symptoms associated with SIBO are abdominal distension, constipation, diarrhea, excess gas, and severe abdominal pain. These signs can be attributed to any number of gastrointestinal ailments, which makes it more difficult to diagnose, and can leave sufferers in chronic pain for months or even years without therapy. When the symptoms of SIBO continue for a prolonged period of time, this can hinder the body's ability to absorb healthy vitamins and minerals. Vitamin and mineral deficiencies can snowball into many other physical illnesses and weaknesses.

SIBO is often the result of other illnesses and deficiencies, such as celiac disease, irritable bowel syndrome, Crohn's disease, low stomach acid, organ dysfunction, diabetes, and scarring from prior bowel surgery. Excessive alcohol intake can also induce SIBO and damage the intestinal lining, further aggravating the already challenging symptoms. This disorder can make way for other frustrating and painful intestinal disorders by wearing away at the intestinal wall, like leaky gut syndrome.

It is difficult to diagnose SIBO due to the host of common complaints that can be attributed to many other gastrointestinal disorders. One effective test that can determine whether or not a patient has SIBO is the hydrogen breath test. In a normal gut, bacteria in the system use carbohydrates and sugars as food, a process that produces gas. Typically, the primary gas associated with a healthy gut is carbon dioxide, with small traces of hydrogen and methane that are used up by bacteria in the colon. In an individual with an unhealthy gut, the hydrogen and methane seep into the lining of the colon and into the blood. The blood stream circulates the hydrogen, transferring it to the lungs and then expelling it through exhalation. Doctors can measure this with the breath test and determine if the patient indeed has SIBO.

Once diagnosed with SIBO or other ailments associated with SIBO, sufferers have a few different options to treat the symptoms that cause such terrible discomfort. The first is a series of antibiotics that lasts a couple of weeks, and while effective, the results tend to be temporary. Another option is probiotics, which are live bacteria added to foods like yogurt and beverages that can help balance the bacteria in the intestines, returning it to normal activity. Over the course of the long term, these can be effective ways of warding off SIBO, but a regimen of lifelong antibiotics should not be the end-all of healing methods if holistic, natural techniques are available.

Whether in conjunction with these treatments or entirely separate of them, a strict change in diet can decrease the likelihood of future flare-ups of SIBO and soothe the gastrointestinal system back to a healthy and balanced state. The SIBO food plan starts by eliminating the kinds of food that cause stress on the intestines and that are the most difficult to digest. This includes foods that are rich in fiber, because the intestinal tract does not easily absorb or digest fibrous foods like some fruits, vegetables, and whole grains. Fermentable foods like dairy products and sugar; beans, lentils and other legumes; certain vegetables such as asparagus, cauliflower, snap peas, artichokes, avocado, and mushrooms; and fruits like prunes, plums, cherries, pears, apples, and dried fruits are also off limits because of the high concentration of sugar.

In addition to this diet change and possible use of probiotics, the addition of gentle bone broth to the SIBO sufferer's diet can be miraculously soothing. The anti-inflammatory qualities of the broth can help restore the digestive lining of the intestines, as well as calm the system and return it to its natural balance. In SIBO support communities and in the medical profession, chicken broth is often recommended as a long-term therapy to help heal and keep symptoms at bay. By incorporating it into a regular diet, the broth can consistently nourish the stressed and aggravated parts of the body and prevent future manifestations of the disorder.

Irritable Bowel Syndrome (IBS)

Irritable bowel syndrome has similar signs and symptoms as SIBO, but is varied in its causes, diagnosis, and risk factors. Fourteen percent of the US population reports symptoms of IBS, and women are two or three times more likely to be diagnosed with it. The most common complaints associated with IBS are constipation, diarrhea, bloating, excess gas, and severe abdominal pain. Nearly one-third of IBS sufferers report low libido or another form of sexual dysfunction. Stress tends to exacerbate the symptoms of IBS, and some studies have indicated that 60 percent of people with IBS also suffer from anxiety and depression. Much of this can be attributed to the interruption of normal lifestyles and the inability to function throughout the day without the illness flaring up and causing intense discomfort. According to other theories, these reactions have more to do with the possible disruption of the brain-gastrointestinal axis and serotonin levels.

While there is no confirmed natural cause of IBS, it is believed that stressful life events, infections, abnormalities in gut flora, and a disruption in communication between the brain and the gastrointestinal tract are most likely to cause it. The use of antibiotics has been shown to increase the likelihood of IBS, and those who have suffered severe gastrointestinal infections are six times more likely to develop it. Other theories suggest that instead of the typically slow muscular movements of the digestive system, IBS creates spastic movements in the colon, causing diarrhea and constipation.

The impetus for finding safe and manageable treatments of IBS, as well as swifter and more accurate diagnoses is significant, but there is plenty of financial incentive as well. It is estimated that in the United States alone, IBS is directly responsible for anywhere between $1.7 and $10 billion in medical costs, and possibly even $30 billion in total for the added expenses associated with absenteeism in the workplace due to the symptoms of IBS. In workers diagnosed with IBS, nearly 35 percent found that the illnesses linked with IBS caused them to lose 13.5 productive hours in a forty-hour workweek.

Treatment of IBS can span a range of diet changes, laxatives, medications, meditative practices, and psychological therapy. The most effective long-term method is a complete shift in dietary practices, which includes removing several different kinds of foods that can cause inflammation and disrupt normal bacterial growth in the intestines from the diet. In some research studies, 70 percent of IBS patients felt relief from transitioning to the FODMAP diet, which excludes many carbohydrates, dairy, and fermentable, sugary food groups associated with inflammation in the intestines and poor nutrient absorption. This diet is the same kind of nourishing regimen that is used to treat other gastrointestinal ailments like SIBO and leaky gut, and for good reason.

The reduction of inflammatory foods benefits the whole body and not just the gut. Foods filled with preservatives and difficult to digest components only exacerbate other issues and ailments in the body, and a return to simple, homemade, natural foods can help soothe the hindrances and maladies caused by these other toxic food groups. The addition of anti-inflammatory foods like bone broth and other wholesome, organic foods can ameliorate the suffering body and help buffer future expressions of serious illnesses like IBS that invade the everyday lives and health of millions of people.

Beauty-Boosting Benefits

Bone broth's most powerful component affects more than just internal health. Collagen does wonders for overall health, and this can translate to how we age as well. The beauty-boosting possibilities of drinking bone broth daily, as well as incorporating it into other parts of your diet, can have incredible effects on skin, hair, and nails. In a time when both men and women spend thousands of dollars on anti-aging treatments—from smoothing wrinkle creams and acne medicines, manicures and pedicures, and shampoo and hair treatments to cosmetics and Botox—a true, home remedy that can help ward off skin-deep signs of aging should be priceless. Instead, it is as inexpensive as making dinner.

Skin and Aging

Beauty is more than skin deep, but caring about your skin and its appearance is not superficial. Healthy skin helps control body temperature, regulate electrolyte balance and fluids in the body, and has innumerable nerve receptors that affect our everyday lives. Protecting this skin through moisturizing, avoiding overexposure to UV rays and using BPA-free sunscreen and coconut oil, and taking extra steps to help prevent skin damage can lead to beautiful skin over many years, but more importantly, it can be life saving.

There are three outer layers that make up the skin: the epidermis, the dermis, and the hypodermis. The epidermis is the outside layer of skin that we can see and touch. It is the protective layer that helps block out pathogens, from dust and dirt to fungi, bacteria, and disease. It is also responsible for keeping water inside the body like its very own swimsuit. This layer of skin is the one that can handle the most wear and tear; it contains no blood vessels, but rather is fed by the layers of skin and capillaries below.

The dermis is the layer just below the epidermis, connected by what is called a basement membrane, which is a tight layer of fibers created by both sections of skin. The dermis is a cushioning layer of connective tissue that is made up of a matrix of collagen fibrils, elastic fibers, and microfibrils. This creates elasticity in the skin, which makes the skin strong and more resistant to wear. It is also part of what makes the skin look smooth, young, and wrinkle-free. The dermis is the layer that hosts the blood vessels that feed and remove waste from other parts of the skin; it also has hair follicles, sweat glands, lymphatic vessels, apocrine glands, and sebaceous glands. The nerve endings in the dermis are what allow us to sense touch and ranging temperatures.

Beneath the top two layers of skin is the hypodermis. This layer is technically not part of the skin, but instead is a protective padding made up of elastin and connective tissue. The hypodermis connects the skin tissue to the bone and muscle below, fueling it with blood vessels and linking it with nerves. This section makes up 50 percent of body fat, as it is the insulator to the body.

As we age, the function of these important parts of the skin starts to break down. In elderly or worn skin, there is a reduction in vascular tissue, as well as a loss in the collagen fibers that are responsible for smooth, strong, and supple skin. This makes the skin very, very thin, causing it to be even more vulnerable to the elements. Wound healing can be four times slower than it can in young skin, blood vessels become fragile and break more easily, and the decrease in function in sweat glands can lead to dry and imbalanced skin. When the strength of skin begins to deteriorate with age, normal habits like plucking, waxing, exfoliating, shaving, washing with medicated cleansers, wearing makeup, and even being out in the sun, cold, or wind can suddenly have serious implications that they did not before. These routine activities can cause cuts, burns, and rashes that take longer to heal and are more difficult to treat. Taking care of your skin over the long haul can help prepare your body for these risks and maintain strong, beautifully smooth skin.

Wrinkles

There is any number of treatments to combat wrinkles, even out complexion, and appear younger. From cosmetics and topical creams to Botox, these can all be pricey and are more often than not temporary solutions. Collagen creams are only moderately effective, as the skin does not absorb the collagen nearly as well as if it were consumed internally. But let's talk about Botox, because it addresses a larger problem with the way that many people are talked into treating illnesses or perceived imperfections with erroneous methods.

Botox injections are effective for the short term in smoothing out wrinkles because it essentially freezes the muscles into staying put. It lasts between three to six months depending on the person, which means it requires two to four visits per year at several hundred dollars per visit. There are a number of snags with this method, the first of which is that Botox does not wholly treat the problem it purports to treat. Botox blocks the nerves that tell the muscles to contract, which is a temporary fix to *certain* kinds of wrinkles. For the space in between your eyes where you furrow your brow, to smile lines and crow's-feet, these are habitual expressions that have caused wrinkles over time. Much in the same way that for people who sleep on their sides, they may have or will begin to notice wrinkle lines down the center of their chests because of the amount of time spent sleeping over the course of a lifetime. The only way to stop those muscle-related wrinkles from forming is to shifts your habits, but the idea of not smiling, squinting, or making any facial expressions *indefinitely* is a bit of a tall order and not particularly enjoyable.

What Botox does not treat, however, are wrinkles that have formed because the loss of collagen in the skin over time. Botox focuses on freezing the muscles of particular problem areas, but can do nothing to replenish the collagen that makes skin look so smooth and young. This means that using Botox is a never-ending, expensive battle that involves repeatedly injecting toxins—specifically botulism—into the face and body. The problem with this approach is that while it can temporarily smooth some wrinkle areas, it is just one more in a growing list of methods and products used to coerce buyers into making repeated, expensive purchases. Not only this, but it encourages a level of acceptance that in order to aid certain health ailments or transform physical imperfections, the only option is to choose chemical treatments over holistic ones.

Hair

The amount of time and money people spend on their hair can run a wide range. From virtually no maintenance at all to flat irons and keratin treatments, to coloring and frequent haircuts, this range in hair care can mean very different things for each person in terms of how healthy their long or short locks may be. A single strand of hair can last between two and six years, so it is important to treat hair well.

For those who dye their hair with traditional dyeing methods, the damage happens swiftly and is only reparable with regrowth. The dye cannot attach to the hair and penetrate its color unless it goes through several protective layers, one of which is the cuticle. The cuticle acts as the armor encasing the hair to shield it from harm. The ammonia in the hair dye increases the pH level of the hair, forcing the cuticle to lift up and allow the color to make its way in. Once the ammonia has broken down the protective barriers, the only thing that can make way for the new color is the peroxide that breaks down the natural hair pigment. After the hair itself has been dyed, the damage from the process has already been done, and hair becomes straw-like and weak. Organic and vegetable dyes are a fantastic, ammonia-free alternative that can help keep hair healthy without sacrificing personal style.

This breakdown of strength and shine in hair is not limited to coloring hair. Age, constant blow-drying, straightening, curling, teasing, and even having too infrequent haircuts can all cause damage and make one's hair look dull, bodiless, and brittle. Many products are available to help aid in this battle, but they can be expensive, ineffective, or redundant. One of the core factors in maintaining hair health has nothing to do with the hair products you purchase, but rather one that comes from within. The collagen supplied by the body helps strengthen the hair and offers a healthy shine. Maintaining collagen levels in the diet is an important way of contributing to hair health, and a decrease in this could have adverse effects. While most people may not be willing to alter their hair care habits significantly when posed with the idea of ditching their blow dryer or covering up grays, incorporating collagen-rich bone broth into a daily diet can help maintain healthy, shiny hair without much effort at all.

Nails

Like the pitfalls of hair care, nails can take a beating as well. As we age, nails can become dull, weak, and grow much more slowly. Aging nails can range anywhere from opaque and hardened, to thick and yellow. Splitting can also occur, which is painful and can cause infection below. While nails act as a protective barrier on the fingertips, they can at times be more penetrable than the skin. Combine this with harsh manicures like shellac, gel, and acrylics that can damage and strip the nail, and the likelihood of sustaining robust, healthy nails reduces exponentially.

Nails require protein, calcium, essential fatty acids, and vitamin A to remain healthy and strong, which can be found in meat, dairy, and legumes. Collagen can also play a part in strengthening nails, just as it does for hair and skin. These elements combined, which are found in the meat sources that produce bone broth, can all work together to help maintain sturdy nails that are less susceptible to splitting or breakage through normal wear and tear or damage from cosmetics.

The Beauty Industry

In considering all of the options available on the market to heal and rejuvenate skin, hair, nails, and other cosmetic imperfections, we must also talk finances. With all of the topical creams, dermatologist visits, spa treatments, laser skin-care solutions, and cosmetics to choose from, the well of money each person sets aside to pay for each of these may very well run dry. According to a recent survey, people across the world spend somewhere in the ballpark of $400 *billion* per year on cosmetics, and 85 percent of those purchases are made by women. A reported 33 percent of men and 35 percent of women use at least one or two beauty products every day, and 17 percent of women use three or four. (Slightly more than half of men do not use a single beauty product in their daily routine, though 1 percent uses six or more.) This is a *lot* of people, which means that even if you make up the percentage of men or women who only uses one prod-uct a day, it is still an inherent part of your routine that requires a serious amount of cash over many years.

When most women replenish the key players of their makeup bags (foundation, mascara, blush, etc.) four to five times per year, this means that the average woman spends roughly $15,000 on cosmetics alone over the course of a lifetime, not including other treatments provided by a doctor, skin care professional, or spa. Fifteen percent of that total is spent on foundation or concealer, and 10 percent is spent on lotion and facial creams. On average, most cosmetic compa-nies mark up the prices of these items by 78 percent, thus building the expecta-tion that certain designer cosmetics have a far higher dollar value, when in truth, these should actually be fairly inexpensive items.

The reality is that cosmetics have an integral role in how men and women feel about themselves, whether it is in the workplace, in romantic relationships, or in how they feel when they leave the house in the morning. Fifty percent of women believe that their appearance affects where they stand and how they are treated in a professional environment, and based on the society we live in, this may very well be true. While many women will probably swear never to part with mascara, doing away with certain elements of a skincare and makeup regimen can be both an emotional and a financial catharsis. Not only can it save thousands of dollars, but it can also empower men and women alike who take part in some form of skincare routine to feel more confident in their own bodies, regardless of what they have put on their face that morning. But how can we go about doing that?

Bone Broth and Beauty

As we have discussed, skin treatments, hair products, and cosmetics are endlessly expensive and can sometimes be damaging to our physical health and emotional wellness. Coupled with the media's constant barrage of pop culture and advertising, the beauty industry can often incite unnecessary and superficial expectations about how individuals should present themselves to the outside world. This unrealistic and arbitrary standard of self-worth can cause depression and unhealthy reactive habits, which circle back to fuel the problem. By focusing on healthful, holistic approaches to your body's well-being, many of these issues can cure themselves. The abundant collagen present in nourishing bone broth has innumerable positive benefits to your health and mind, but also for your skin. Just as getting the recommended daily dose of calcium can help maintain and protect your bones, nails, and other parts of the body as you age, the collagen, vitamins, and minerals in bone broth can further replenish your body's own collagen and keep skin, hair, and nails looking great well down the line. Pairing this with a generally healthy diet, exercise, and an awareness of which things are worth putting into your body and which are not, bone broth can have incredible, lifelong, glowing effects on your outer beauty as well as on what is within.

Bone Broth Health and How Other "Trends" Stack Up

What Bone Broth Does for Us as Eaters and Home Cooks

With every health trend, whether it is juicing, coconut oil, detox cleanses, gluten-free dieting, or another movement of the moment, it can be difficult to sift through all of the different messages coming our way. We live in a society that is constantly on the go, and taking care of ourselves can be exhausting, particularly when there are so many conveniences—from fast food to prepared meals to boxed mixes that cut the time of cooking considerably. While this is an understandable concession of a busy lifestyle, we pay for it later with excess weight, nutrient deficiency, and myriad illnesses and ailments that can make life pretty miserable.

With all of these different diets competing with one another, nailing down the exact benefits of each and applying it to your own diet can be a daunting task. Going gluten-free can be a wonderful way to rid your body of many inflammatory food products, but sometimes it can be easier to ask "Is that gluten-free?" than question whether even a gluten-free swap is truly healthy for you or just labeled that way. Similarly, juice cleanses can offer myriad benefits from antioxidants and energy boosters, but if it is made with non-organic fruits and vegetables, you may just be drinking an elixir of sweetly flavored pesticides and chemicals from the farming process. Many green juice products, for example, contain large portions of fruit juice to sweeten the vegetable taste, but contain scads of fructose that can cause spikes and drops in blood sugar level. Businesses in the food industry can just as easily slap on a "gluten-free" or "green juice" label to a product without having to reconcile other empty nutritional elements, and this can be very damaging to consumers who rely on honest labeling to make their food selections.

What consumers, health enthusiasts, and chronic illness sufferers who are looking to make healthy changes should take away from the trend of the moment is twofold: first, that it should never be a *trend*. Nutritious eating is about healthy lifestyle changes as a whole, and while some movements like the Paleo Diet appear as though they are here to stay while others have long since passed, it is because Paleo has been able to accomplish what other nutritional movements have not. It has encapsulated what healthy eating truly is by weeding out the preservative-filled and processed foods that many people have become so used to seeing on store shelves or passively nuking in the microwave after a long day. The second is that the marvel diet or ingredient of the moment is never *just* about that one ingredient, but rather what that ingredient can mean as a tool to open the door to a rejuvenated, energetic, and healthy new lifestyle full of opportunity. Too much of something is never a good thing, whether it is water, sunlight, or even bone broth, but added in balanced amounts to a daily lifestyle can be the health awakening that you have been waiting for.

So what makes bone broth different? Bone broth is a return to our roots. As a species, hunting, gathering, and preparing meals based on animal meat were what made us thrive. Boiling the meat and bones of animals for soups and stews was perhaps the founding culinary practice of our survival. The health benefits of bone broth are innumerable, but the exercise of preparing it is what makes bone broth truly unique. Unlike many other popular health trends, the emphasis on drinking and cooking with bone broth is not so much about restricting a particular food group, but rather on having special awareness of the kinds of foods that we choose to put into our bodies. The practice of selecting healthy bones from local farmers, organic butchers, and organic food sources is the first step along this path, because it manifests a desire to take control over the healthfulness of the food that ends up on the dinner table.

While cooking bone broth can seem intimidating based on the long hours it can often require, modern conveniences like pressure cookers and slow cookers mean that you do not have to sit around monitoring the stove all day. Making bone broth is as simple as adding healthy bones, water, and vinegar to a pot and letting the goodness from the bones cook out into a rich broth over many hours. Once you have nutrient-filled bone broth in your kitchen, drinking it daily and using it as a base for meals can become as routine as preparing a morning cup of coffee or boiling a pot of water. Taking a step back and preparing a meal that is truly made from scratch can help us better understand the cost of convenience in other foods that we have commonly accepted into our diets. The practice of preparing bone broth can manifest into other elements of our cooking as well, from selecting vegetables and spices that boost energy, revitalize our whole system with good vitamins, minerals, and nutrients, and detoxify our bodies by ridding them of all of the foods that weigh us down and contribute to illnesses. The most important aspect to remember of this nourishing approach to cooking and eating is that it is not that hard. With an investment in time-saving kitchen appliances, incorporating bone broth into a regular routine is completely within reach, if not incredibly easy.

Higher Energy

The extra boost in energy is just a few daily cups of bone broth away. Not only is the elixir packed with nutrients, minerals, protein, and vitamins that can replenish your system, but also in practice, drinking bone broth can replace some of the drinks that make us lethargic, unmotivated, and less likely to be active. Sugary energy drinks, sodas, and too much caffeine can stimulate momentary rushes of energy, but more often than not, they are followed by intense, regrettable energy crashes and adrenal fatigue. Not only this, but these kinds of beverages are filled with preservatives, chemicals, and coloring agents that can have severe health consequences, from weight gain and illnesses, all the way to cancer.

Drinking bone broth is a warm pick-me-up, but its nutrient and protein base sparks energy and jump-starts metabolism. Pair this with supercharged stews and soups made from bone broth, and the medley of vitamins, rich minerals, and nutrition yields a healthy, balanced diet that keeps your system from experiencing inflammation, digestive problems, and other stressors related to diet that can prevent us from getting up and moving. Studies show that individuals who take an active role in food preparation and health-conscious eating are more likely to exercise and relish activity. Some may chalk this up to be a personality trait, but the reality is that if your body feels good from the nutritious foods you put into it, you are more likely to want to get on your feet and use that body.

Better Sleep

Most Americans suffer from sleep deprivation in some form or another. According to the National Center on Sleep Disorder Research at the NIH, 30–40 percent of adults in the United States report symptoms of insomnia, and 10–15 percent of those people suffer from chronic insomnia. What's more, the National Sleep Foundation has found that 38 percent of Americans awake from sleep feeling unrested, with others in that group experiencing tossing, turning, and an inability to return to sleep if woken. This is a very real problem because the stress on the body associated with lack of sleep can creep into the day, causing fatigue, low energy, and headaches, and can lead to more arduous health problems down the line. Sleep disorders are often associated with obesity, hypertension, diabetes, stroke, depression, cardiovascular disease, poor work performance, memory lapses, impaired cognitive function, gastrointestinal ailments, irritability, and anxiety. Excess weight and inactivity can cause disruptions in breathing during sleep, causing sleep apnea and other sleep disorders.

The benefits of bone broth to sleep are multifaceted. The first is that with healthy nutrition and bone broth as a part of an active lifestyle, individuals can reduce obesity and gastrointestinal-related sleep deprivation and have more restful nights. Additionally, the amino acid glycine has been found to facilitate the sleep cycle. Its interaction with brain receptors may be responsible for limiting muscle movement during REM sleep (rapid eye movement), increasing serotonin levels, and lowering core body temperature. Bone broth is rich with amino acids, including glycine, which can help transition the body into healthier and more restorative sleep cycles.

Battling a Cold

Chicken soup has been the trusted home remedy for cold and flu season for generations. While the reasons behind this have long been anecdotal, recent studies have indicated that chicken soup can inhibit neutrophil migration, which typically leads to inflammation. The combination of fats and antioxidants in soup made from a whole chicken work together to achieve other health benefits, but the anti-inflammation qualities of chicken soup can deter a number of nutritional deficiencies and sicknesses. Additionally, sipping the warm broth stimulates nasal clearance. Drinking the broth throughout the duration of a cold can help improve painful symptoms of the upper respiratory tract.

Fitness and Recovery From Injury

Sports and fitness have long been closely linked with high-protein diets, and for good reason. Protein provides energy and helps build muscle, but as a society, we tend to rely on lean cuts of meat and protein powders. While this can have many short-term benefits in the way of muscle building and strength, neglecting the other parts of the meat that include joint pieces, cartilage, and marrow is a missed opportunity for many other reasons. These lesser-chosen parts of the animal provide the vitamins, amino acids, minerals, and fatty acids that lean cuts do not. This can lead to vitamin deficiency and cause harm over the long term.

This is where bone broth comes in. The gelatin in bone broth contains many important, conditionally essential amino acids that can help athletes train, compete, and repair the wear and tear on their bodies that can result from intense physical exertion. Gelatin supplements have even been associated with over 200 percent higher performance output in athletes. Studies have shown that 15 grams of glycine paired with exhaustive exercise can increase dexterity, rebuild muscle tissue, bolster muscle strength, and fend off exhaustion. Glutamine, another conditionally essential amino acid present in bone broth, can support the immune system, reduce muscle atrophy, and help the body recover from fatigue faster. When the body is overworked, particularly through athletics and intense training, muscles release glutamine to help make up for this exhaustion. When this happens, the muscles weaken. Drinking bone broth as an exercise supplement can replenish this glutamine so that this kind of negative result is never a problem.

When faced with injury, athletes can do astonishing damage. Constant training and strain on the body can break down cartilage and joints, tear ligaments, and add intense strain on the skeletal frame. With daily cups of bone broth, these joints, connective tissues, and bones receive constant nourishment and protection of amino acids and anti-inflammatory agents that can make injury less likely. In the case of injury, however, the typical response is for the athlete to take NSAIDs like ibuprofen to suppress inflammation and decrease pain. Dependency on these kinds of medicines can lead to worn stomach lining. Instead, a holistic approach with bone broth can reduce injury-associated inflammation and speed up the healing process. The LA Lakers' nutrition consultant—a physician—has been prescribing bone broth to the players for years with phenomenal results. When the prognosis for a severely sprained ankle seemed to mean that Kobe Bryant would not play for the foreseeable future, bone broth brought him back in two games. Bone broth can offer athletes and people who live active lifestyles a healthy buffer, aiding in muscle strength, safeguarding bones and muscle tissue, and soothing recovery in the face of injury.

Weight Loss

The most healthful elements of bone broth relate to the lifestyle, eating habits, and body healing that it promotes, but it is also a great tool for weight loss.
No individual should look to bone broth alone as a replacement for meals. Enhanced bone broth drinks like the "Energy Tonic" in this book have the benefit of additional fats that release nutrients slowly and consistently into the bloodstream. Bone broth contains many beneficial vitamins, nutrients, and minerals, but it is not so packed with nourishment that it can meet a day's needs in any of these categories by itself. Weight loss should be managed in a responsible way, meaning that it should include exercise and meals full of heart-healthy, anti-inflammatory, and clean foods. At the same time, broth is the perfect source of nutrition to satisfy and curb hunger until the next meal rather than unhealthy but convenient snacks.

At this point in time, the population of the United States is experiencing a terrible obesity crisis. More than 65 percent of Americans are overweight, and 35 percent of those individuals are obese. The distinction between the two depends on weight as it relates to body mass index, or BMI. For a person who is five foot nine inches, being "overweight" means someone who weighs between 169 and 202 pounds and who has a BMI between 25.0 and 29.9. "Obese" would be 203 pounds or higher with a BMI of 30 or more. This can cause countless life-threatening or life-altering sicknesses, from heart disease and diabetes to infertility and cancer. Lifestyle changes and shifts in the functionality of the commercial food industry are the only way to reverse these numbers, but the process for one individual alone can seem insurmountable. Many diets are aimed at people looking for a quick weight loss miracle, but oftentimes these can become expensive, challenging to make into a routine, and, frankly, boring to keep up day in and day out.

The perks of adding bone broth into your diet are that it is low-calorie on its own, inexpensive over the long term, simple to make into a daily occurrence, and has dozens of associated recipes for tonics, soups, stews, recipes, and even cocktails to make it an exciting part of your day. The caloric content of one cup of beef, chicken, or fish bone broth rests between sixteen and thirty calories, depending on the ingredients added to the blend. This number goes up significantly for commercially sold broths, which can range between fifty-five and two hundred calories based on the additives. Without added salt, bone broth contains very little sodium and about 1.3 grams of fat.

Let's look at the health content of other popular beverages and snacks that many people could replace with bone broth each day, compared with the recommended daily allowance:

Nutritional Category	Recommended Daily Intake
Calories	2,000–2,500
Sugar	25g (6 teaspoons)–37.5g (9 teaspoons)
Fat	44g–78g
Carbohydrates	225g–325g
Sodium	2,325g

Smoothies and Pressed Juice

In a popular juice product, a nine-fruit smoothie containing the juice of one and a half apples, one-third cup cherries, one-fourth peach, one-fourth pear, three-fourths orange, one-sevenths mango, four blackberries, and one strawberry contains 45 grams of sugar. While these fruits have many health benefits individually, the sugar content is nearly *double* the recommended amount for daily intake. This drink also contains three hundred calories, which is 15 percent of the recommended daily intake on a two thousand-calorie diet. More often than not, the average person thinks little about the caloric content of beverages, which can lead to excess calories when combining that smoothie with coffees, sodas or sugary drinks, and alcoholic beverages that the average individual may consume in a given day. While juicing is a great way to get nutrients and vitamins from organic produce, a good rule of thumb is to eat organic fruit and juice organic vegetables. Otherwise, the result is an excess of sugar that can negate the other benefits of eating healthy fruit.

Pumpkin Spice Latte

No sooner do the leaves begin to change than the pumpkin spice lattes start brewing at every local and nationwide coffee shop. This latte is a comforting treat for a chilly day, but many people get hooked on adding it to their breakfast routine as a way to start their day or indulge in later in the afternoon. A traditional pumpkin spice latte when made with whole milk and whipped cream yields 410 calories, 150 fat calories, 51 carbohydrates, and 48 grams of sugar. This is 20 percent of the day's calorie intake and double recommended amount of sugar—all on a beverage that offers no other nutritional benefit. Indulging in these kinds of treats every once in a while is okay for healthy individuals. Making them routine is where health issues come into play, and it is generally a good idea to avoid these sugary, caloric drinks.

Plain Latte

A non-fat latte without whipped cream is a significantly better choice than the above latte, but it is not without its failings. With 130 calories, zero fat, 19 carbohydrates and 18 grams of sugar (prior to any added sugar), it is under the recommended sugar intake for the day, but not by much. Many people swear by their daily dose of caffeine, but there are other ways to get bursts of energy than by partaking in a milky cup of espresso.

Blueberry Muffin

The classic breakfast for many people on the go, a blueberry muffin is an American staple. This delectable luxury is misleading because most people have learned to think of it as a breakfast food rather than a dessert. When it comes down to it, eating a blueberry muffin and foods like it in the morning is as nutritionally good for you as eating a cupcake. A typical blueberry muffin from a national coffee chain has 460 calories, 60mg of cholesterol, 450mg of sodium, and 44 grams of sugar. You are quite literally better off eating a chocolate-frosted doughnut (but don't). Not only is this a huge chunk of your daily calorie intake and almost double the sugar, it is packed with preservatives, white flour, and other processed ingredients that can cause inflammation and other long-term side effects of unhealthy eating.

Granola Bar

A granola bar may actually be the best option on this list, but that is not saying much. A typical whole grain oat and raisin granola bar is about 90 calories, 0mg of cholesterol, 80mg of sodium, and 7 grams of sugar. This is much more in line with the amount of calories, sugar, and cholesterol that should be in a snack; however, most commercially sold granola bars are made with corn syrup, wheat flour, artificial flavors, and even "cookie pieces" (this is an actual ingredient in one popular brand). Whole oats can be a hearty part of a breakfast that can help curb hunger, but only if they are completely natural and without additives and preservatives.

Pita Chips

So delicious! And also so terrible for you. The serving size on pita chips will make anyone feel sad about themselves, because it only allots about 10 chips. By design, these kinds of snacks are meant for binge eating, and the nutritional info associated with them tends to be misleading. Very few people are able to limit their intake to the given amount, and in this case, this means at least 130 calories, 270mg of sodium, and 19 grams of carbohydrates. While baked pita chips certainly are the lesser of evils compared to processed orange chips or puff snacks, they still heavily rely on inflammation-causing ingredients like wheat flour.

Bone Broth

Drinks and snacks that people tend to rely on each day for a boost of energy can often be the exact reason they struggle with fluctuating or constant weight problems. Many commercially sold beverages, breakfast items, and snacks all contain high amounts of calories, sugar, and sodium, but are often marketed as healthy or normal go-to foods. While indulging in these foods is a natural part of life, they can become a burden when struggling with weight and gastrointestinal ailments. By replacing these daily snacks or wake-up beverages with a few cups of bone broth, you can not only reduce unwanted calories, sugar, and sodium in your diet, but also have an energy-boosting, warming treat that makes you feel satiated and content between meals. If boredom is a concern, enriching bone broth can be made into a variety of healthy tonics and soothing hot drinks that will cure whatever ails you.

Adding Bone Broth to Your Daily Routine

At first glance, cooking bone broth can seem intimidating. The process of making bone broth is actually very straightforward and does not have to take whole days or even many hours. The first thing is to remember that brewing broth is as old a culinary practice as cooking hot meals is, so whether you are well versed in the kitchen or just learning, making homemade broth is nothing if not human nature. The difference today is that we have numerous options for cooking, many of which cut out the need to monitor the stove for hours on end. Particularly with a pressure cooker, bones will break down as if they have been cooking for days without the hassle. Once you have mastered the few easy steps of cooking bone broth regularly, there are many different ways to incorporate it into your diet.

Drink a Cup for Breakfast

Nourishing bone broth is packed with protein and energy boosters. Whether you are someone who needs a big, well-rounded breakfast to start your day or someone who subsists strictly on coffee until lunchtime, adding bone broth to your breakfast regimen will be a seamless transition. Heat up a cup of bone broth and sip it while you get ready for your day, while you read or watch the news, or take it to go in a coffee thermos on your way out the door. For many people who drink coffee or tea with sugar in the morning, the initial rush is inevitably followed by a crash, which sets off jitters, derails your energy levels, and inhibits your ability to focus. Warming broths like the Energy Tonic in this book will be a comforting wake-up boost each day, and the protein in the broth will help you feel full and satisfied until your next meal.

Replacing a Snack or Afternoon Coffee

Do a snack swap. Instead of reaching for granola bars to fend off hunger or grabbing an extra cup of coffee to wake you up during the 2 p.m. lull, heat up some revitalizing bone broth. Bring containers of the broth to work or have it in the refrigerator at home for when hunger pangs between meals set in. The protein will give you a burst of energy that snack foods will not, and it is a low-calorie, nourishing alternative to some of the empty calories that can offset a person's generally healthy diet.

Rotate Your Broth Recipes

Chicken broth, beef broth, fish broth, or mixed broths—there seem like so few options. In reality, rotating the kinds of broth you drink or use in recipes can make all of the difference. The savory tastes of each kind have something special to offer, and adding different herbs and spices to cooked broth can change the flavor dynamic enough so that drinking broth never gets old. Whether you add ginger to chicken broth or turmeric to beef, these subtle hints of flavor create the kind of flavor depth that makes each cup unique and satisfying.

Soothing Tonics

Drinking bone broth straight is delicious on its own, but cooking up soothing, tea-like tonics are a comforting, revitalizing alternative. The tonics recipes in this book can help ramp up libido, warm you on a cold day, and help with inflammation. From Chinese herbs to curry broth, these hot beverages are endlessly drinkable.

Cocktails

Yes, cocktails. Drinking bone broth with alcohol is not a new invention. Even back in the early 1950s, the Detroit-based Caucus Club was brewing up a "Bull Shot." This drink served piping hot is the spicy and savory response to a Hot Toddy, mixed with vodka, bone broth, lemon, and spices like hot sauce and cayenne pepper. For the Bloody Mary drinkers of the world who love a bit of salt and spice in their alcoholic beverages, bone broth will be a fitting addition to cocktail lists and has huge flavor potential. See the "Brocktails" section for step-by-step instructions on how to mix up your own broth-based cocktails at home.

Use It as a Base

Broth-based meals like soups and stews are delicious and satisfying, but not every day is a soup day. For times like these, use bone broth as seasoning or to hydrate food when a recipe typically calls for water. You can use it as a flavorful liquid base for preparing anything from steamed vegetables to "mashed"

recipes like cauliflower or sweet potatoes to gravies and rich sauces. The versatility of homemade broth means that it will never go to waste.

Get Cooking!

This may seem like an obvious step, but there are so many ways to cook with bone broth. From pho noodles to hearty stews, to gravies and hot drinks, the possibilities for cooking meals with bone broth are endless. The recipes in this book provide simple, healthful recipes to utilize the broth while enjoying all different styles of soups, stews, and other meals.

Gelatin Supplements

Bone broth is a great way to get gelatin into your diet, but there are also supplements that can be consumed in addition to or within bone broth recipes to make them extra potent. There are two kinds of supplements that can be used: gelatin and collagen hydrolysate.

Powdered gelatin made from grass-fed animals can be added as a thickening agent in many types of food whether you are making homemade marshmallows and Jell-O or adding it to your bone broth. Gelatin powder is hot water-soluble, meaning that it can only be dissolved in hot water or it will not gel. It should be noted, however, that daily doses of gelatin powder can be harsher on the system for people with weaker digestive tracts. It should only be consumed in small quantities when cooking and not overused.

Collagen hydrolysate is easier on the system than gelatin powder is. While it shares the same benefits as gelatin, it is not interchangeable as a cooking agent. Collagen hydrolysate will not make foods gel the same way as gelatin will, and it is cold water-soluble. This means that you can mix collagen hydrolysate powder with any beverage, yogurt, smoothie, shake, and soup.

When adding new supplements to your diet, it is important to start off slowly and to follow the recommended doses on the label. Most people start off with one-half to one tablespoon per day of collagen hydrolysate and increase bimonthly thereafter, up to two to three tablespoons per day. You can do this by mixing it in with yogurt or a shake in the morning and ending your day with it in a hot drink or soup. One cup of daily bone broth with it also yields similar results.

PART 2: PREPARATION

Choosing Your Bones

The first and most important step of cooking bone broth is choosing the right bones. This comes down to both the type of bone that will release the highest amounts of gelatin, nutrients, and flavor into your bone broth as well as where that bone came from. As discussed previously, grass-fed, pasture-raised, free-range, and wild-caught sources are the only animals that can produce the healthy benefits of bone broth. Using grain-fed beef or farmed fish will only exacerbate existing health issues due to the contaminants in the animals' environments and unhealthy feed given to them over the course of their lives.

Choosing Bones for Flavor and Nutrition

While selecting ethical resources for your meat and fish products can sometimes be challenging and more expensive, the reasons for choosing the kind of organic bones that will provide the best flavor and nutrition is significantly clearer. Bones that have high cartilage content, marrow, and gelatin are by far the most important bones to include in your broth because you will see the most nutritional benefits.

Beef shank, oxtail, knucklebones, and feet are all concentrated sources of gelatin, which will be released over the course of the long cooking process for making broth. The same goes for pork products for parts like the knucklebones and feet. Including the parts of the animal that are not always used in the modern diet allows us to make use of nose-to-tail style cooking. While the meat can be cooked in meals, the leftover bones can make nutrient-rich broth that does not let any part of the animal go to waste.

In poultry, the carcass you end up with after roasting a chicken, turkey, or duck is not the only resource for great bone broth; chicken feet and chicken heads are packed with gelatin and good nutrition. While this may come off as unseemly for many people who are not used to seeing chicken feet on their cutting boards, it is both healthful and makes use of the whole animal without wasting parts.

Beef, pork, and poultry bones will have greater potential for releasing gelatin into your broth, but fish bones offer flavor variation and an opportunity not to waste the leftover bones and shells after a meal. The whole carcasses, including the heads, of non-oily fish like snapper or sole make for delicious fish broth, and so too do shrimp and other shellfish.

If you are cooking bone broth for the first time, start off with an animal whose flavor profile is one you most enjoy cooking and eating with. If you are naturally a chicken soup lover, use a whole roasted chicken in your cooking, including the wings and feet. These will bring out the best gelatin content and have flavor potential that you can drink and then use in your cooking. If you are a beef stew connoisseur, use beef bones in your first batch, including marrow and oxtail that will be both nutrient dense and flavorful. A broth with mixed bones, from chicken and turkey bones to pork knuckles and beef marrow, will build complex flavors for a great drinkable broth.

Saving Bones

Preparing bone broth with freshly roasted or raw bones that you get from a butcher, local farmer, or supermarket is always a great choice, but you can also use the bones that you have left over from cooking meals. Any time you roast a chicken, prepare bone-in beef, or roast a whole pig—for the ambitious—wrap up the leftover bones and store them in the freezer. The next time you decide to prepare bone broth, you can use these saved bones and still get the same fantastic nutritional benefits as if you had prepared it during the same day. This method prevents waste by presenting the opportunity to use the whole animal, whether it is nose-to-tail or beak-to-tail feather.

Vinegar and Citrus

One crucial ingredient that you will see over and over in bone broth recipes is some sort of vinegar or citrus. The acid in either vinegar or citrus helps extract the minerals in the bones, infusing your broth with great nutritional value. A mild vinegar-like apple cider or rice wine will help draw out the minerals without being too overpowering in flavor as with traditional white vinegar. Citrus, particularly lemon, will also help with this.

It is important to note that vinegar can enhance the free glutamates that are released in the broth cooking process. While a long boil over the course of several days will also release more free glutamates, vinegar does the same thing over a shorter period of time. If you are sensitive to free glutamates, vinegar may exacerbate this problem.

Ditch the *Mirepoix*

Many bone broth recipes call for *mirepoix*, or a mixture of chopped white onion, peeled carrots, and sliced ribs of celery. It seems only natural to want to add these ingredients to bone broth recipes; after all, they are the vegetables everyone relies on to enhance homemade chicken noodle soup. The recipes in this book do not call for *mirepoix* for one very important reason: it is completely unnecessary!

Vegetables break down at a *much* faster rate than bones, so by the time your broth is ready, any nutritional value and flavor from these ingredients will have long since lost their vigor. Bone broth's flavor appeal and nutritional benefit originate from the animal bones being cooked over the course of many, many hours, not from the broken-down *mirepoix*. Add these aromatic vegetables and other herbs and spices to your soups *after* you prepare the broth so that you can get the full nutrition and comforting flavors.

This makes for a significantly simpler recipe without the waste in vegetables and the time it takes to prepare them. For excellent, hearty bone broth, all you need are the gelatin-rich bones, water, apple cider vinegar to release the minerals, and salt to taste.

Cooking Methods

There are several cooking appliances that can be used to make bone broth, but the preparation is the same across the board. Cooking broth in a pressure cooker can have nutrient-rich broth in your cup or recipes in less than three hours, and slow cookers do all the work over hours and even days with little need to check up on them. Preparing bone broth over the stove may be the closest to how generations past cooked broth, but it is also the method that requires the most responsibility. Leaving the broth unattended on a burning stove can lead to all sorts of unfortunate disasters, so it is important to actively oversee its progress throughout the cook time.

The recipe below offers instructions for each kind of cooking method and can be applied to any type of bone, from marrowbones, poultry carcasses, backs or necks, pig knuckles, ham hocks, to pig or chicken feet and even hooves.

Easy Bone Broth Recipe

Ingredients:
5 lbs. bones, raw or cooked cooked leftovers
5 quarts water
2 tbsps apple cider vinegar
1 tbsp salt, to taste

Method:
1. In a stockpot, pressure cooker, or slow cooker, add bones.
2. If raw, brown if desired to increase flavor. If using bones with fat, such as chicken backs, drain oil after browning.
3. Add water, salt, and vinegar, cover, and bring to boil.
4. Reduce heat to a simmer and cook, covered, 1–3 hours in a pressure cooker, 24–48 hours in a slow cooker, or 12–24 hours stovetop. Add water as needed to stovetop or slow cooker, and skim fat and film as it cooks.
5. Strain out bones and add salt to taste.

Cooking Ratio

If you would like to make a different quantity than the recipe listed above, use the ratio of one pound of bones to one quart of water, with one teaspoon of salt and one-half tablespoon of vinegar per pound of bones.

Why Your Bone Broth Will Not Gel

One of the best markers of nutrient-rich bone broth is that it congeals into a gel-like substance once cooled in the refrigerator. While perhaps unappetizing at first, the gel indicates that the gelatin in the bones, joints, and cartilage pieces that you used during the cooking process has properly made its way into your bone broth. This leads to a super-healthy broth that incorporates all of the health benefits discussed in this book. If the broth does not congeal or thicken when cooled, there are a few things you can do on your next batch that can make all the difference:

1. Add more bones and gristle! You might not have enough of the right kinds of bones in your broth if it is not gelling. Go heavy on the chicken feet, chicken wings, marrowbones, feet or hooves, chicken or fish heads, and even a whole poultry carcass. Using these parts specifically will ensure that the broth you are brewing will be the most potent in nutrients as possible.

2. Use the *right* kind of bones. If you cheated and used non-organic beef, poultry, pork, or fish bones, you know where the problem is. It is extremely important that the bones used to make bone broth are from healthy animals. If the animals are malnourished and vitamin deficient, the bone broth will be too.

3. Make sure the heat reaches a boil. The broth will cook at a low temperature for the majority of the time when using a slow cooker or the stove, but it is important that the heat reaches a boil at the beginning.

4. Acid. Specifically in vinegar, acid will help bring out all of the gelatin and minerals in the bones. If you went light on the vinegar on your first attempt, be sure to add more in your next. While it can smell strong when you first add it, a tablespoon or two more will not make a substantial change in the flavor or aroma of the overall broth. If you have a strong distaste of vinegar or are wary of using too much vinegar that might exacerbate any sensitivities you may have to free glutamates, then substitute the vinegar for citrus like lemon juice.

5. Let it cook longer. If you are preparing your bone broth in a slow cooker or over the stove, try to keep it simmering for as long as possible. Anything less than eight hours means that the gelatin has not had enough time to release into the broth. A least a day, even two, will be your best bet for the highest quality bone broth.

Storage

Straining the Broth

This is a simple but important step. Once your broth is finished, use a large mesh sieve to strain out the remaining bones. Dispose, re-use, or pulverize the bones in a high-powdered blender to feed pets. However, the latter should only be done if the bones are thoroughly blended to prevent injury from sharp edges. Straining the broth will catch all of the smaller pieces that have broken down, leaving only the rich broth behind. Most mesh sieves have plastic edges that can rest on a stockpot or large measuring container, which allows you to use both hands to carefully strain the broth from the pot you cooked everything in.

Storage Jars

Glass containers like mason jars and Pyrex bowls are ideal for storing broth. Large mason jars are great sizes for portioning broth for soups, and small glass jelly or sauce jars are the perfect size for individual cups of drinking broth. These can be reused over and over again and washed in the dishwasher, making cleanup and continuous broth storage incredibly easy. Metal lids on mason jars have a tendency to rust over time, so it is a good idea to purchase plastic replacement lids that screw right onto mason jars. For glass jars that close with clamps, replacement rubber gaskets for worn out ones can be found at any hardware store or online.

Freezing Broth

When freezing bone broth in glass jars, the most important thing to remember is to leave at least two inches between the broth and the lid. Liquid expands when frozen, which can cause full jars to shatter. In just the same way that hot beverage glasses right from the dishwasher can break when filled with cold liquid or ice, breakage can happen when transferring the jar from hot to cold locations. Be sure to allow the broth to cool to room temperature before storing it in the freezer, or refrigerate for a day and remove the fat from the top prior to freezing. This will minimize shatter risk and make the thawing process significantly easier.

Ice Trays

A great time saver and recipe trick, pouring reduced bone broth into ice trays and freezing them is a resourceful method to season or add moisture to any meal. Whether you are roasting vegetables or making brown rice, bone broth cubes can add just the right amount of flavor. Take a couple of cubes of reduced bone broth and heat them in a saucepan prior to incorporating them into your cooking. Cover the trays with plastic wrap or parchment paper so that they remain separate from other ice trays in your freezer.

Dehydrated Broth

Dehydrated broth is an incredible way to make your broth portable or to prepare your own powdered bouillon seasoning. Whether you are traveling and still want to get in a daily cup of bone broth or you are going on a camping trip and want to make soup, dehydrated broth is a good way to accommodate these needs.

This process is time consuming, but can be well worth it. Prior to dehydration, the broth will need to be reduced so that it is thick enough to spread evenly on flat dehydrator sheets. The length of time will vary depending on the amount of broth used, but ten cups of broth will cook down to about one cup of reduced broth over several hours. The next step of the process calls for the same kind of food dehydrator that one would use to make dried fruit and jerky at home. Once the broth is dried, it can be broken into pieces and pulverized in a coffee grinder, high-powered blender, or smashed by hand in a plastic bag with a wooden mallet. Dehydrated broth is shelf stable and can be saved in mason or spice jars. About one tablespoon of powdered broth yields one cup of rehydrated broth, depending on your preferences for taste.

Method:
1. Remove the solidified fat off the top of broth that has cooled in the refrigerator for several hours. Discard or store the fat in the refrigerator to be used as cooking grease.
2. In a large stockpot, place the broth on medium to medium-high heat until it reaches a heavy simmer. Let it cook down for several hours (about six) or until the broth has reduced to a thick consistency. You may need to lower the heat gradually to make sure it does not burn or adhere to the pot.

3. Pour in thin layers (⅛ inch) onto parchment-lined dehydrator sheets.
4. Dehydrate at 155 degrees for 14–24 hours, or until brittle.
5. Break into pieces and pulverize in a coffee grinder or high-powered blender until powdered.

PART 3: RECIPES

Introduction

It is my desire that by now you are thoroughly jazzed by the idea of making your own bone broth. You hopefully realize what a simple process it is, how economically sound the ingredients are, and that the health benefits may be life transforming for you. While I will be content if you decide to make broth itself, I also want you to feel like you can easily incorporate it into your daily life in health-promoting, flavorful ways. I've created fifty recipes that run the gamut in terms of ingredients, uses, and tastes, but they have a few things in common that are important to me: they are made with whole foods, they are all gluten free (with the exception of a replaceable vodka and an organic Worcestershire sauce I recommend in the brocktail section), most do not contain grains, most are Paleo compliant (though you may wish to switch out olive or avocado oil for lard or coconut oil), they are chock full of veggies and other healthful ingredients, most are low-glycemic and safe for diabetics, and most are anti-inflammatory.

When you shop for ingredients for any of these recipes, please consider your body, the bodies of whomever you are feeding, and the planet: buy organic ingredients and well-raised meat and bones. I haven't noted to use organic items specifically because to me that's a given. If you must choose which organic ingredients to get due to budget, always prioritize animal products and any produce that if not organic may be GMO. Remember that you can't poison your way to good health, but you can healthfully eat your way there. You'll also notice that for shelf-stable ingredients I only recommend jars, not cans; as I said on Food Network's *Chopped*, I only use cans to feed cats. Ingredients in jars are subject to far fewer additives and have none of the chemical lining concerns, such as BPA, that cans do.

I hope you find these recipes, which are meant to be springboards for your own imagination and not steadfast rules to cook by, inspiring and thought provoking. Thank you for joining me on the journey of combining food and wellness!

Bone Broths: Why It's OK to be Basic

There are two distinct bone broth camps: the purists who insist on nothing but bones and water and the flavorists who want to throw in all possible forms of produce and herbs to take up space and make bone broth taste more like soup. I'm not one to tell you not to make your food fun, but I find the addition of excessive aromatics to be just that: excessive. You will hardly notice the flavors of onion, celery, or garlic that has cooked for twenty-four hours, and its nutrient value by the end of cooking will be nil. I like to keep my broths simple and add the flavors after the fact, either by using the broth as a soup base or by adding an ingredient or two for a wellness tonic, unless I am making broth for a specific function (which has its own recipe section after this one).

The only additions I find necessary for basic broths are apple cider vinegar to help extract the minerals out of the bones and salt. Salt adds additional minerals, provided you are using Himalayan or another pink salt such as Real Salt, and it makes tasting the broth a better experience. That said, you don't want to add very much until the broth is done, as the water reduction could easily result in an over-salted broth. I have included an aromatic ingredient in each bone broth recipe that will create a symbiotic flavor profile with the meat used, for those who prefer flavored broths, but they are optional.

Basic Beef Bone Broth

This is the most commonly used of all bone broths, and its nutrient profile is the densest; grass-fed beef contains CLA, ALA, Omega-3, and has strong anti-inflammatory properties. The flavor is easy to work into any meaty recipe once the broth is made, and it has a classic taste.

Serves 8–10

Ingredients:
5 lbs. beef marrow bones, raw or cooked leftovers
5 quarts water
2 tbsps apple cider vinegar
1 tbsp salt
Optional: two bay leaves

*If you would rather make a different quantity, use the ratio of 1 pound of bones to 1 quart water, with 1 teaspoon salt and ½ tablespoon vinegar per pound of bones.

Method:
1. In a stockpot, pressure cooker, or slow cooker, add bones.
2. If raw, brown if desired to increase flavor.
3. Add water, salt, and vinegar, cover, and bring to boil.
4. Reduce heat to a simmer, and cook, covered, 1–3 hours in a pressure cooker, 24–48 hours in a slow cooker, or 12–24 hours on a stove top. Add water as needed to stove top or slow cooker, and skim fat and film as it cooks.
5. Strain out bones and add salt to taste.

Basic Chicken Bone Broth

There is a reason that "chicken soup for the soul" is an expression, as well the namesake for a bestselling collection of books. Chicken broth is universally comforting and has excellent immune-boosting properties. The flavor is distinct, yet can easily be drawn into the background of other recipes to add an umami quality.

Serves 8–10

Ingredients:
5 lbs. chicken necks, backs, and/or feet, raw or cooked leftovers
5 quarts water
2 tbsps apple cider vinegar
1 tbsp salt
Optional: 3 sprigs of thyme

*If you would rather make a different quantity, use the ratio of 1 pound of bones to 1 quart water, with 1 teaspoon salt and ½ tablespoon vinegar per pound of bones.

Method:
1. In a stockpot, pressure cooker, or slow cooker, add bones.
2. If raw, brown if desired to increase flavor. If using backs, drain oil from pan after browning.
3. Add water, salt, and vinegar, cover, and bring to boil.
4. Reduce heat to a simmer, and cook, covered, 1–3 hours in a pressure cooker, 24–48 hours in a slow cooker, or 12–24 hours on a stove top. Add water as needed to stove top or slow cooker, and skim fat and film as it cooks.
5. Strain out bones and add salt to taste.

Basic Lamb Bone Broth

L amb: it may be adorable, but it's also chock-full of B vitamins, zinc, and even more CLA than beef. Though the taste is mild, the scent is strong and has what some might consider an off-putting level of "game" meat smell. Despite that, people love its gentle flavor, and it makes a great vehicle for all sorts of spice combinations.

Serves 8–10

Ingredients:
5 lbs. lamb marrow bones, raw or cooked leftovers
5 quarts water
2 tbsps apple cider vinegar
1 tbsp salt
Optional: four springs of mint or two whole cloves

*If you would rather make a different quantity, use the ratio of 1 pound of bones to 1 quart water, with 1 teaspoon salt and ½ tablespoon vinegar per pound of bones.

Method:
1. In a stockpot, pressure cooker, or slow cooker, add bones.
2. If raw, brown if desired to increase flavor.
3. Add water, salt, and vinegar, cover, and bring to boil.
4. Reduce heat to a simmer, and cook, covered, 1–3 hours in a pressure cooker, 24–48 hours in a slow cooker, or 12–24 hours on a stove top. Add water as needed to stove top or slow cooker, and skim fat and film as it cooks.
5. Strain out bones and add salt to taste.

Basic Fish Bone Broth

Though most people never notice, the gelatin from fish bones is used in commercial products from marshmallows to gummy candies. While this is one of the less good-looking types of broth to make, mostly according to those who don't like to be stared at by their food, fish has such a different nutrient profile from poultry or red meat that it is an excellent way to change things up.

Serves 8–10

Ingredients:
5 lbs. fish heads and carcasses, raw or cooked leftovers
5 quarts water
2 tbsps apple cider vinegar
½ tbsp salt
Optional: several sprigs of dill

*If you would rather make a different quantity, use the ratio of 1 pound of bones to 1 quart water, with 1 teaspoon salt and ½ tablespoon vinegar per pound of bones.

Method:
1. In a stockpot, pressure cooker, or slow cooker, add bones.
2. If raw, brown if desired to increase flavor.
3. Add water, salt, and vinegar, cover, and bring to boil.
4. Reduce heat to a simmer, and cook, covered, 1–3 hours in a pressure cooker, 24–48 hours in a slow cooker, or 12–24 hours on a stove top. Add water as needed to stove top or slow cooker, and skim fat and film as it cooks.
5. Strain out bones and add salt to taste.

Basic Mixed Poultry Broth

Chicken is the perfect poultry go-to, but there is plenty to be gained by changing out your bird bones. Duck is an excellent source of zinc and selenium, and turkey is chock-full of B vitamins. Because both duck and turkey have a distinctly different taste than chicken, combining the three will yield a flavorful broth that still has a comforting, "normal" flavor.

Serves 8–10

Ingredients:
5 lbs. chicken, duck, and/or turkey bones, raw or cooked leftovers
5 quarts water
2 tbsps apple cider vinegar
1 tbsp salt
Optional: several sprigs of rosemary

*If you would rather make a different quantity, use the ratio of 1 pound of bones to 1 quart water, with 1 teaspoon salt and ½ tablespoon vinegar per pound of bones.

Method:
1. In a stockpot, pressure cooker, or slow cooker, add bones.
2. If raw, brown if desired to increase flavor.
3. Add water, salt, and vinegar, cover, and bring to boil.
4. Reduce heat to a simmer, and cook, covered, 1–3 hours in a pressure cooker, 24–48 hours in a slow cooker, or 12–24 hours on a stove top. Add water as needed to stove top or slow cooker, and skim fat and film as it cooks.
5. Strain out bones and add salt to taste.

Functional Broths: When Being Basic Isn't Enough

Inasmuch as I don't think it's worthwhile to throw half the contents of your produce bin into your stockpot for twenty-four hours, I do acknowledge that there are times when plain broth just won't do the trick. Whether you're feeling inflamed or you're looking for an energetic pick-me-up, a couple quick additions to your broth can up its game to new plateaus. Because nutrients and flavors get lost with extended cooking, I recommend adding the enhancers very late in the cooking process. If cooking on the stove top, add them in during the last hour. In the slow cooker, add them with about two hours to go. If using a pressure cooker, wait until the broth has finished. Once you have de-pressurized the pot and opened the lid, add the enhancers to infuse as the broth cools. If you are going the stove top or slow cooker route, leave the additions in large pieces, and if adding after de-pressurizing, cut into small pieces or grate. These recipes will make an entire batch of broth with one enhanced function; if you prefer a single serving for your cause, please see the section of tonic recipes.

Beautifier

While all bone broths contain collagen and help contribute to your body's own collagen production, this broth is the fast track there. Chicken and pig feet are dense with it, and lycopene-rich red foods such as tomatoes and hot peppers help your body create more. The flavor of these bones is surprisingly mild, so the tomatoes actually play a larger part here in taste than one would anticipate.

Serves 8–10

Ingredients:
3 lbs. chicken feet
3 pig feet
1 lb. tomatoes, halved
5 quarts water
2 tbsps apple cider vinegar
1 tbsp salt
Optional: one hot red pepper, with or without seeds, halved

*If you would rather make a different quantity, use the ratio of 1 pound of bones to 1 quart water with 1 teaspoon salt, and ½ tablespoon vinegar per pound of bones.

Method:
1. In a stockpot, pressure cooker, or slow cooker, add chicken and pig feet.
2. If raw, brown if desired to increase flavor.
3. Add water, salt, and vinegar, cover, and bring to boil.
4. Reduce heat to a simmer, and cook, covered, 1–3 hours in a pressure cooker, 24–48 hours in a slow cooker, or 12–24 hours on a stove top. Add water as needed to stove top or slow cooker, and skim fat and film as it cooks.
5. Add tomatoes, and hot pepper if using, with one hour left on a stove top, two hours left in the slow cooker, or at the end of de-pressurizing if using a pressure cooker.
6. Strain out bones and tomatoes and add salt to taste.

Inflammation Reducer

All broth made from grass-fed meat and wild fish will help lower inflammation, but if it's currently a problem you are dealing with, you may wish to amp up your defenses and tackle it as fiercely as possible. Packed with ginger, turmeric, and sweet potatoes, this recipe is like a chill pill for your system.

Serves 8–10

Ingredients:
5 lbs. beef or lamb marrow bones, raw or cooked leftovers
5 quarts water
6 inches ginger root, sliced into ½-inch rounds
1 medium sweet potato, cut into quarters
4 fresh turmeric roots, sliced lengthwise
2 tbsps apple cider vinegar
1 tbsp salt

*If you would rather make a different quantity, use the ratio of 1 pound of bones to 1 quart water, with 1-inch ginger, 1 turmeric root, ¼ sweet potato, 1 teaspoon salt, and ½ tablespoon vinegar per pound of bones.

Method:
1. In a stockpot, pressure cooker, or slow cooker, add bones.
2. If raw, brown if desired to increase flavor.
3. Add water, salt, and vinegar, cover, and bring to boil.
4. Reduce heat to a simmer, and cook, covered, 1–3 hours in a pressure cooker, 24–48 hours in a slow cooker, or 12–24 hours on a stove top. Add water as needed to stove top or slow cooker, and skim fat and film as it cooks.
5. Add sweet potato, ginger, and turmeric with one hour left on a stove top, two hours left in a slow cooker, or at the end of de-pressurizing if using a pressure cooker.
6. Strain out all solids and add salt to taste.

Immunizer

We've already established that chicken broth is great for immunity, but there is no reason not to take things a little further and create a broth expressly designed to knock colds and flus on their butts, rather than them knocking you on yours. Utilizing an array of standard immunity boosters like garlic and mushrooms, it may be pungent but it definitely tastes better than Nyquil. As a bonus, one of the main antioxidants in mushrooms, ergothioneine, won't get destroyed by the long cooking.

Serves 8–10

Ingredients:
5 lbs. chicken backs, necks, or other bones, raw or cooked leftovers
5 quarts water
2 tbsps apple cider vinegar
1 tbsp salt
2 bulbs garlic, sliced in half through the center
4 oz. dried shiitake mushrooms, reconstituted
2 oz. dried maitake mushrooms, reconstituted
6 sprigs fresh oregano

Method:
1. In a stockpot, pressure cooker, or slow cooker, add bones.
2. If raw, brown if desired to increase flavor. If using chicken backs, drain oil after browning.
3. Add water, salt, and vinegar, cover, and bring to boil.
4. Reduce heat to a simmer, and cook, covered, 1–3 hours in a pressure cooker, 24–48 hours in a slow cooker, or 12–24 hours on a stove top. Add water as needed to stove top or slow cooker, and skim fat and film as it cooks.
5. Add remaining ingredients with one hour left on a stove top, two hours left in a slow cooker, or at the end of de-pressurizing if using a pressure cooker.
6. Strain out all solids, and add salt to taste.

Digestive Broth

Bone broth is considered excellent for digestion because of how well the gelatin can soothe and heal your intestines. Adding beets is like taking a digestive aid along with the broth because beets contain betaine, which stimulates bile production. Their greens are bitter, and bitter foods stimulate the production of digestive juices in the stomach. Zucchini has mild laxative properties and helps stabilize blood sugar.

Serves 8–10

Ingredients:
5 lbs. salmon, chicken, or beef bones, raw or cooked leftovers
5 quarts water
2 medium zucchini, sliced into ¾-inch rounds
3 medium beet roots, cut into ½-inch cubes
Greens from 3 beet roots, sliced if desired (can be kept whole)
1 tbsp salt
2 tbsps apple cider vinegar

*If you would rather make a different quantity, use the ratio of 1 pound of bones to 1 quart water, with a half zucchini, 1 small beet root with greens, 1 teaspoon salt, and ½ tablespoon vinegar per pound of bones.

Method:
1. In a stockpot, pressure cooker, or slow cooker, add bones.
2. If raw, brown if desired to increase flavor.
3. Add water, salt, and vinegar, cover, and bring to boil.
4. Reduce heat to a simmer, and cook, covered, 1-3 hours in a pressure cooker, 24-48 hours in a slow cooker, or 12-24 hours on a stove top. Add water as needed to stove top or slow cooker, and skim fat and film as it cooks.
5. Add zucchini and beets with one hour left on a stove top, two hours left in a slow cooker, or at the end of de-pressurizing if using a pressure cooker.
6. Strain out all solids and add salt to taste.

Mood Booster

If you have tried bone broth before, you already know that it can provide a surprisingly hefty amount of bio-available energy. With the additions of lemongrass for a citral-laden lift and asparagus for a hit of folate and tryptophan, the feel-good nature of broth is made supernatural here.

Serves 8–10

Ingredients:
5 lbs. chicken, salmon, or beef bones, raw or cooked leftovers
5 quarts water
1 tbsp salt
2 tbsps apple cider vinegar
6 inches lemongrass, broken or cut in half
1 bunch asparagus, cut into thirds

*If you would rather make a different quantity, use the ratio of 1 pound of bones to 1 quart water, with 1 inch lemongrass, 4 stalks asparagus, 1 teaspoon salt, and ½ tablespoon vinegar per pound of bones.

Method:
1. In a stockpot, pressure cooker, or slow cooker, add bones.
2. If raw, brown if desired to increase flavor.
3. Add water, salt, and vinegar, cover, and bring to boil.
4. Reduce heat to a simmer, and cook, covered, 1–3 hours in a pressure cooker, 24–48 hours in a slow cooker, or 12–24 hours on a stove top. Add water as needed to stove top or slow cooker, and skim fat and film as it cooks.
5. Add lemongrass and asparagus with 1 hour left on a stove top, 2 hours left in a slow cooker, or at the end of de-pressurizing if using a pressure cooker.
6. Strain out all solids and add salt to taste.

Veggie Blendies: The Natural Next Step

Phase one of any serious gut health plan (like the Specific Carbohydrate Diet) involves consuming large quantities of bone broth to heal. Next comes the incorporation of vegetables, usually in blended form along with broth. The intro phases of some diets will have you strain them, but that isn't necessary unless you are suffering severe digestive distress. I have collected ten of my favorite recipes that bring vegetables and broth together in beautifully nutritious harmony.

Roasted Butternut Blendie Soup

Butternut squash has more potassium than bananas and enough beta-carotene to reduce your risk of cancer. It's also super tasty. Better yet, all you have to do to make soup out of it is cut it in half, scoop out the seeds, roast it, and blend. No need for complex cubing, and the caramelization from roasting makes for a satisfying flavor.

Serves 6–8

Ingredients:
1 large or 2 small butternut squashes
1 tsp salt
½ tsp freshly ground pepper
2 tbsp olive oil
4 cups beef or lamb broth
¾ tsp ground sage

Method:
1. Preheat oven to 375 degrees F.
2. Halve squash lengthwise and remove seeds.
3. Sprinkle squash with salt and pepper.
4. Place butternut squash halves skin side down in a baking dish and drizzle with olive oil.
5. Bake until tender, approximately 50 minutes.
6. Once removed from the oven and cooled slightly, scoop squash meat out of skin and place in blender.
7. Blend squash, broth, and sage until smooth. Add salt if desired.

Roasted Bell Pepper Blendie Soup

Vitamin C, vitamin E, lutein, lycopene—bell peppers are the nutritional over-achievers of the vegetable world. For best nutrient variety, choose an assortment of red, orange, and yellow peppers. Green ones are great for you too, but they don't taste nearly as good, and combining them with anything red or orange won't yield a pretty result. Stick to combos on the warm side of the rainbow for best results.

Serves 6–8

Ingredients:
8 medium bell peppers
2 tbsps olive oil
1 tsp salt
4 cups beef or lamb broth
½ tsp smoked paprika
½ tsp freshly ground pepper

Method:
1. Preheat oven to 375 degrees F.
2. Place whole bell peppers on a parchment-lined baking sheet and drizzle with olive oil.
3. Bake until tender and with blackened spots, approximately 45 minutes.
4. Remove from oven and cover with additional piece of parchment for 30 minutes.
5. Peel skins off and discard seeds. Reserve all juices.
6. Blend peppers, juices from roasting, broth, and seasonings until smooth. Add salt if desired.

Parsnip & Pear Blendie Puree

For most of my life, it has been difficult to remember the difference between parsnips and turnips; both seemed like boring white root veggies to me, and I didn't have much interest in either. Then one day I made a parsnip puree for a client, and they've been secure in my mind ever since. (Hint: they are the ones that look like white carrots, not the round things with purple edges.) Parsnips are anti-fungal and rich in vitamins K, B, and E. Their delicious sweetness is due to their high sugar content, but that's fine in moderation. Pears add a nice contrast of flavor and have flavanols to fight aging.

Serves 4–6

Ingredients:
2 tbsps grass-fed butter
6 large or 8 small parsnips
1 tbsp dried dill
2 medium pears, any type
2 cups chicken broth
1 tsp salt
Freshly ground black pepper

Method:
1. Melt butter in a large saucepan.
2. Add parsnips and dill and sauté until parsnips are slightly softened, 3–5 minutes.
3. Add remaining ingredients, cover, and bring to a boil.
4. Reduce heat to a simmer and cook until parsnips are tender, about 15 minutes more.
5. Cool slightly, and then blend until smooth.

Sweet Potato & Apple Blendie Mash

Reminiscent of something you would eat on Thanksgiving, the combination of sweet potatoes and apples with chicken broth is heavenly. We've discussed that sweet potatoes are anti-inflammatory, and of course they are high in beta-carotene too. Apples are high in fiber, thus helping prevent gallstones, and their quercetin content boosts immunity.

Serves 4–6

Ingredients:
2 tbsps grass-fed butter
2 medium sweet potatoes, cut into ½-inch cubes
2 large, firm apples such as Granny Smith or Fuji, cut into ½-inch cubes
1 ½ cups chicken broth
1 tsp cinnamon
¾ tsp salt

Method:
1. Melt butter in a large saucepan.
2. Add sweet potatoes and sauté until lightly golden, about 5 minutes.
3. Add remaining ingredients, bring to a boil, and cover.
4. Reduce heat to a simmer and cook, covered, until apples and sweet potatoes are tender, about 10 minutes more.
5. Remove from heat and use a potato masher or other tool to tenderize and help mash potatoes and apples. Remove half of mixture and blend until smooth, with additional broth or water if needed, and then reincorporate. Final result should be somewhere between a hash and applesauce.

Thousand Cloves of Garlic Blendie Soup

Admittedly, the name is a bit hyperbolic, but it is impossible to say exactly how many cloves of garlic are in this soup because the amount of cloves per bulb varies. It is fair to say, though, that four bulbs worth of garlic kind of feels like a thousand cloves. Thankfully, roasting them mellows out their flavor dramatically without losing too much of their allicin, the sulfur compound that makes garlic so healthful.

Serves 6–8

Ingredients:
4 bulbs garlic
2 tbsps olive oil
1 tsp dried marjoram
1 tsp dried oregano
6 cups lamb broth
¾ tsp salt
Freshly ground black pepper to taste

Method:
1. Preheat oven to 375 degrees F.
2. Slice tops off garlic and pour ½ tablespoon olive oil over each. Sprinkle dried herbs on top.
3. Roast until golden and soft, about 35 minutes.
4. Let cool, then blend with broth until smooth. Add salt and pepper to taste.

Super Greens Blendie Soup

Green smoothies have been all the rage for years now. Take that green drink to a broth-tastic place by gently cooking your veggies in broth and then blending for digestive ease. You can't go wrong no matter which hearty greens you choose; all contain nutrients to help you stay young, good looking, and with good enough vision to see your beautiful self in the mirror.

Serves 6–8

Ingredients:
2 bunches leafy greens, such as kale, collards, chard, mustard, or dandelion
6 cups beef broth
1 tbsp grass-fed butter
¾ tsp salt
½ cup fresh parsley
Juice of ½ lemon

Method:
1. Chiffonade greens into manageable pieces.
2. Heat broth in a small stockpot until simmering.
3. Add greens and salt and cook, covered, for 5 minutes or until greens are wilted and softened.
4. Let cool slightly and then blend with remaining ingredients. To prevent browning, chill quickly and add the lemon juice.

Sunchoke Vichyssoise

A sunchoke is an amazing vegetable that tastes like an artichoke and a potato had a baby. I use them in place of potatoes, which are the norm for vichyssoise, because they are so much healthier and create a creamy soup without needing dairy. They are high in inulin, a form of prebiotics that act as food for probiotics. In typical vichyssoise fashion, they are paired with leeks, a mellow member of the onion family that is also high in sulfur but lacks the sharp bite of its onion and garlic cousins.

Serves 6–8

Ingredients:
1 ½ lbs. sunchokes, peeled if desired and sliced into ½-inch rounds
2 large leeks, sliced into 1-inch rounds
4 cloves garlic, roughly chopped
6 cups chicken or mixed poultry bone broth
2 tbsps olive oil
2 tbsps dill weed
1 tbsp ground sage
Salt and pepper to taste

Method:
1. Heat oil in a large pot and then add all ingredients except for broth.
2. Cook for 5–10 minutes until veggies are slightly wilted and golden.
3. Add broth and cook for 25–30 minutes until sunchokes are soft.
4. Cool slightly, then blend until smooth and season to taste.

Chilled Avocado Blendie Soup

I am of the opinion that avocados are one of the most delectable foods in existence. If you agree with me, you will love this blended soup. If you don't, you still might like it because it is creamy, mild, and has a little Spanish flair by way of dried coriander. Avocados have tons of fiber—11 grams each—plus plenty of protein and healthy fats.

Serves 4-6

Ingredients:
3 ripe large avocados
1 cup yogurt
2 ½ cups chicken or fish broth
1 tsp salt
2 tsp dried coriander
¼ tsp ground white pepper

Method:
1. Scoop avocados out of skin and place in blender.
2. Add all other ingredients and blend until smooth.

Cauliflower Blendie Puree

I don't necessarily think you should try to fool people into eating healthier food, but I will say that I pass this dish off as mashed potatoes regularly. It's a little lighter than a standard mash, but it is so creamy and fluffy that people often will just assume it is made from potatoes. I'd be lying if I said I didn't let them believe it sometimes. Cauliflower contains choline for brainpower, glucosinolates for detox, and a huge variety of antioxidants.

Serves 4–6

Ingredients:
1 large head cauliflower
1 cup chicken broth
3–4 tbsps grass-fed butter
¾ tsp salt
Freshly ground black pepper to taste

Method:
1. Cut one head cauliflower into florets. Any size is fine, as long as they are fairly even so they cook at the same speed. Place florets in a pot with the cup of broth. Cover and turn onto high.
2. Once boiling, turn down to low and let steam for about ten minutes. Once cooled enough to handle, put steamed florets in a high-powered blender or food processor with 3–4 tablespoons butter, broth from cooking (which contains all the nutrients the cauliflower lost) and salt and pepper to taste. Blend until smooth and creamy.

Chili Verde Blendie Sauce

I have used this tomatillo sauce as everything from a salsa to a stew base. As a salsa, it's ready once blended, and for a stew, just simmer a stew meat in it for a few hours and season with additional salt if needed. Though they are a nightshade, tomatillos contain only low levels of inflammatory alkaloids and are high in potassium for healthy blood pressure, niacin for energy, and antioxidants to fight cancer.

Serves 6–8

Ingredients:
1 ½ lbs. tomatillos, husks removed and halved
1 cup beef or chicken broth
1 onion, chopped
1 Anaheim pepper, chopped
4 cloves garlic, minced
2 jalapeños, chopped and seeded if desired
¾ cup cilantro leaves
1 tsp salt

Method:
1. Heat a large saucepot over medium high heat.
2. Add all ingredients except cilantro and bring to a boil.
3. Reduce heat to a simmer and cook, covered, until ingredients are soft and tomatillos have given out their juice.
4. Uncover and reduce over medium heat until most of the liquid has evaporated, 10–15 minutes.
5. Let cool slightly and blend with cilantro until the texture of salsa.

Playing the Standards: My Takes on Old Favorites

If you have broth on hand, you will likely want to use it for some standard "normal food" recipes like chili or tomato soup. Dishes like those are an easy way to feed bone broth to your family, since they won't even notice they are consuming it, and it is also an easy way for you to consume more of it yourself. I've gathered a host of high-performance standard players and have given them gentle makeovers so that they are as good for you as possible.

Chicken Soup with Quinoa Dumplings

Quinoa dumplings may not be the new black, but they have been my version of matzoh balls for some time now. They're a little denser than matzoh balls, but are still light enough for soup, mild in flavor, and a healthful alternative to wheat-based matzoh. Quinoa has more amino acids than nearly any other vegetarian food does, and though generally considered a grain, is actually a seed.

Serves 6–8

Ingredients:
Soup:
6 cups chicken broth
1 onion, chopped into ½-inch dices
2 stalks celery, chopped into ½-inch slices
2 carrots, chopped into ½-inch coins
2 cooked and shredded chicken breasts
4 cloves garlic, minced
2 tbsps olive oil or butter
2 tbsps onion powder
1 tsp garlic powder
1 tbsp dried parsley
1 tbsp dried rosemary
1 tsp marjoram
Salt to taste: approximately 1 tsp
Black pepper to taste: approximately 8 grinds of a pepper mill

Quinoa Dumplings:
1 cup quinoa flour
2 large eggs
1 tsp dried dill
1 tbsp olive oil
¾ tsp salt

Method:
1. For Quinoa dumplings, combine all ingredients. Stir well and set aside.
2. Heat oil or butter in a large pot over medium-high heat.

3. Add all ingredients except chicken and cook until fragrant, about five minutes.
4. Add broth, and bring to a boil.
5. Drop quinoa dumplings by tablespoonfuls into pot once broth is boiling. Use two spoons to create quenelles, or use one spoon and a finger to create rounder balls. Recipe should create 15–20 dumplings, depending on size.
6. Let soup and dumplings cook for about fifteen minutes, or until dumplings are done (they will float when ready, just like matzoh balls) and vegetables are fork tender.
7. To serve, remove dumplings from pot and trim off any funky-looking edges. Place shredded chicken and dumplings in the pot to warm before serving.

Minestrone Soup

Minestrone is a crowd pleaser; it has something for everyone, and it's a complete meal in a bowl. I have found that no one ever notices that brown rice pasta isn't regular wheat pasta in here, so I don't tend to mention it. Feel free to add some meat for an even bigger kick of protein than the beans and veggies already provide.

Serves 6–8

Ingredients:
1 tbsp extra virgin olive oil
2 shallots, chopped into ¾-inch pieces
3 cloves garlic, minced
1 tbsp salt
1 tbsp basil
1 tbsp oregano
1 jar organic tomato paste
6 cups chicken, lamb, mixed bone, or beef broth
2 cups leafy greens such as spinach or kale, chiffonaded
3 cups root vegetables such as celery root, cut into ¾-inch cubes
2 cups broccoli, chopped
2 cups cooked kidney beans
3 cups al dente cooked brown rice pasta

Method:
1. Heat olive oil in a soup pot on medium high.
2. Add shallots and garlic and sauté until lightly golden, about five minutes.
3. Add herbs and salt, then sauté for another several minutes.
4. Add tomato paste until paste has darkened, 2–3 minutes.
5. Add broth and all veggies.
6. Bring to boil, then lower heat to low and cook for 20–30 minutes or until veggies are fork tender.
7. Add beans and pasta and heat through.

Beef Pho

Shirataki noodles are the unsung hero of the noodle world. With about fifteen calories, no net carbs, and no fat, they are a moderately nutritious filler food made of a fiber derived from konjac yams that absorbs any flavor you add to it. They can be found near tofu in grocery stores, and some brands contain tofu. Not being a fan of soy, I prefer the ones that don't, such as NoOodle.

Serves 4–6

Ingredients:
2 packages shirataki noodles
6 cups beef broth
Bouquet garni bag: 2-inch piece of ginger, 2 cloves, 1 star anise, 6 peppercorns
1 lb. sirloin, very thinly sliced
1 tbsp fish sauce
2 tbsps coconut sugar
Garnishes: 1 cup each bean sprouts, cilantro leaves, sliced scallions, lime
    wedges, thinly sliced Thai chili peppers

Method:
1. Cook shirataki noodles according to package instructions and set aside.
2. Bring beef broth to a boil in a pot and add bouquet garni bag.
3. Reduce heat to a simmer and infuse for 15–20 minutes.
4. Remove bag and add sirloin, fish sauce, and coconut sugar. Turn off heat.
5. Stir briefly to cook steak.
6. Add 1 cup noodles to each bowl and top with soup. Garnish as desired.

Chicken Pho Ga

Fun fact: pho is a common breakfast food in Vietnam. While I prefer a butter-filled tonic herb drink for breakfast myself, there is no contesting that soothing chicken broth, protein-packed roast chicken, and fresh herbs would make a healthful and filling beginning to the day.

Serves 4–6

Ingredients:
2 packages shirataki noodles
6 cups chicken broth
Bouquet garni bag: 2-inch piece of ginger, 6 coriander seeds, 1 cinnamon stick, 1 cardamom pod, 6 black peppercorns
1 roasted chicken
2 tbsps fish sauce
2 tbsps coconut sugar
Garnish: 1 cup each bean sprouts, mint, basil, thinly sliced Thai chilies, onion

Method:
1. Cook shirataki noodles according to package instructions and set aside.
2. Bring chicken broth to a boil in a pot and add bouquet garni bag.
3. Reduce heat to a simmer and infuse for 15–20 minutes.
4. As broth simmers, shred meat from whole roasted chicken into bite-sized pieces.
5. Remove bag and add fish sauce and coconut sugar. Turn off heat.
6. Add chicken meat to pot and heat through.
7. Add 1 cup noodles to each bowl and top with soup. Garnish as desired.

Apricot Lentil Stew

Lentils are a health food go-to: high in fiber, folate, and iron, they are even more nutritious than beans. Sadly, I tend to find them lacking in excitement, so I've been adding dried fruit to my lentil preparations since my first chef job at age nineteen. Apricots provide the punch I think these guys need while also adding calcium, manganese, and copper for strong bones.

Serves 6–8

Ingredients:
1 tbsp grapeseed or other neutral oil
1 onion, chopped
1 carrot, chopped
2 tsp cumin seeds
2 cloves garlic, minced
1 tbsp Frontier chili powder
1 ½ cups green lentils
5 cups beef, lamb, mixed, or chicken broth
1 cup dried apricots, chopped
1 tsp salt
1/3 tsp cayenne pepper
Fresh mint to garnish, torn into rough pieces

Method:
1. Heat oil in a soup over medium high heat.
2. Add onion, carrot, cumin seeds, and garlic; sauté for five minutes.
3. Add chili powder and cayenne pepper and sauté for additional several minutes.
4. Add lentils, salt, and broth; bring to a boil.
5. Reduce heat to medium-low and cook, covered, for ten minutes.
6. Add apricots and cook additional 15–20 minutes or until lentils are soft and have begun to break down.
7. When serving, garnish with fresh mint leaves.

Mixed Bean Chili

If you have been making bone broth, you've clearly learned patience. Why not continue your patient quest to make food from scratch by cooking your own beans for chili? It is much simpler than you may realize, and you won't be consuming any scary BPA or other chemical can linings. Beans are high in fiber, protein, and assorted minerals. Frontier's chili powder blend is a bit different than most; it contains spices that other brands don't, such as cloves, that will add a unique depth of flavor.

Serves 6–8

Ingredients:
1 ½ cups each dry kidney and pinto beans, or 1 cup each dry kidney, pinto, and black beans
3 jalapeños, 1 separated
1 medium onion, quartered
6 large cloves garlic, 2 cloves separated
2 tbsps grapeseed or other neutral oil
1/3 cup Frontier chili powder
2 tbsps oregano
1 tbsp cumin
1 tbsp salt, or to taste
1 tsp chipotle powder
3 tbsps apple cider vinegar
1 7 oz. glass jar Bionaturae Organic tomato paste
4–5 cups beef or mixed bone broth
1 32 oz. glass jar Bionaturae Organic pureed tomatoes (if it is spring or summer, you can puree enough tomatoes to make 32 oz.)

Method:
1. Soak beans overnight in plenty of water. Drain and rinse.
2. Chop jalapeños, onion, and garlic into desired sizes. I do a moderately fine dice and like to use both green and red chilies.
3. Sauté chilies, onion, and garlic in grapeseed oil in pressure cooker or large pot until lightly colored.
4. Add all spices and sauté until fragrant.
5. Deglaze pot with cider vinegar.

6. Add tomato paste and cook until it darkens.
7. Add beans, broth, and pureed tomatoes.
8. Put top on pressure cooker and let cook for 35–45 minutes once pressurized. Alternately, cook in regular pot on medium-high for 50–70 minutes until beans are tender. Add additional broth if needed once chili is cooked.

Shrimp Risotto

Risotto made with brown rice may seem like an impossibility due to how long brown rice needs to cook, but it's actually very straightforward with one simple trick: you cook the rice for 30 minutes with half the cooking liquid before you begin the "risotto" process of slowly stirring in liquid and breaking down the grain to get the requisite creaminess. The end result is 100 percent as creamy as risotto made with Arborio, and much better for you. While it would be even healthier to use black or red rice, the results would be a bit more darkly colored. If that doesn't concern you, either black "forbidden" rice or heirloom red rice would be my top choices.

Serves 4–6

Ingredients:
2 tbsps olive oil
6 cups chicken or fish broth, hot
1 onion, diced
4 cloves garlic, minced
1 tsp dried basil
1 ½ cups brown rice
1 ½ tsps salt
Freshly ground black pepper to taste
1 cup white wine
1 lb. shrimp: ½ lb. chopped, ½ lb. kept whole
1 cup grated Parmesan cheese
½ cup thinly sliced scallions
1 tbsp fresh thyme leaves
1 tbsp butter

Method:
1. Heat a medium-sized pot over medium-high heat and add olive oil.
2. Heat broth in a small pot and keep on low.
3. Add onions, garlic, and basil and sauté for 5 minutes.
4. Add brown rice, salt, and pepper and sauté for 1–2 minutes, until rice is sticky.
5. Add ½ cup white wine and 3 cups hot chicken broth.

6. Cover, bring to a boil, reduce to a simmer, and let cook for 30 minutes. Stir occasionally.
7. Begin adding remainder of wine and hot broth a half cup at a time, with lid uncovered, stirring frequently, until rice is cooked al dente and creamy. Add chopped shrimp and cook through.
8. Once shrimp is cooked through, remove from heat and add Parmesan, scallions, and thyme.
9. In a small pan, heat butter over medium-high heat and sauté whole shrimp until just cooked, about 1 minute per side. Garnish bowls of risotto with whole shrimp.

Tortilla Soup

While I don't particularly endorse eating corn due to its inflammatory nature, I do understand that billions of people love it. If you are going to eat corn, eating it with bone broth will help to offset its inflammatory ways. Tortilla soup is a favorite of my clients, and there is no frying needed; the deep, rich tortilla flavor comes not from chips, but from roasting the rounds in the oven.

Serves 6–8

Ingredients:
8 corn tortillas
3 tbsps neutral oil such as avocado or grapeseed
2 tsps salt
1 onion, diced
3 cloves garlic, minced
2 bell peppers, diced
2 jalepeños, seeded if desired and diced
½ tsp chipotle powder (warning: spicy!)
6 cups chicken or mixed poultry broth
1 jar organic crushed tomatoes
2 cups cooked and shredded chicken
½ cup cilantro leaves for garnish

Method:
1. Preheat oven to 375 degrees F.
2. Drizzle tortillas with 2 tablespoons of oil and 1 tsp salt on a baking sheet and roast until golden and fragrant, 5–10 minutes.
3. Heat a stockpot over medium-high heat and add remaining tablespoon of oil. Sauté onions, garlic, peppers, and chipotle powder until softened, about 5 minutes.
4. Add broth, remaining salt, and tomatoes, and bring to boil.
5. Reduce to simmer and cook about 15 minutes until color has darkened.
6. Break tortillas into 1–2 pieces by hand, or cut with a knife. Assorted sizes are fine.
7. Add tortillas and chicken to pot, remove from heat, and garnish with cilantro.

French Onion Soup

While you could give this soup the old-fashioned bread and cheese topping treatment, it is so delicious that there is really no need. The secret is the long, slow caramelization of the onions with the help of a little honey and balsamic vinegar to heighten flavors.

Serves 4–6

Ingredients:
2 tbsps butter
4 sweet onions, very thinly sliced
2 tbsps honey
2 tbsps balsamic vinegar
6 cups beef or lamb broth
1 ½ tsps salt
Freshly ground black pepper to taste

Method:
1. Melt butter in a medium sized stockpot over medium-high heat.
2. Turn down to medium-low and add onions.
3. Stir frequently and allow to caramelize for 15 minutes, until lightly golden. If browning too quickly, lower heat.
4. Add honey and balsamic and sauté, stirring often, for another 10 minutes or until deeply golden.
5. Add broth, salt, and pepper and bring to a simmer for serving.

Tomato Soup

Not only do you not need Campbell's to make tomato soup, you don't need ketchup, canned tomatoes, or evaporated milk, either. This modern take on a classic recipe uses fresh produce roasted to charred-up goodness.

Serves 6–8

Ingredients:
2 ½ lbs. tomatoes, quartered, seeds and juice removed
3 cups mixed poultry, lamb, or chicken broth
1 onion, sliced into ¼-inch slivers
4 cloves garlic, cut in half
2 tbsps olive oil
2 tsps dried Italian herbs
1 bay leaf
1 ½ tsp salt
Garnish: 1 cup grated Parmesan

Method:
1. Preheat oven to 415 degrees F.
2. Combine all ingredients except for broth in a large baking dish.
3. Roast until edges of tomatoes and onions are very dark, about 45 minutes, stirring every 15 minutes.
4. Let cool, then blend with broth. Garnish with Parmesan when serving.

A Little Bit Cheesy Spaghetti Squash

It's just like spaghetti!" is a claim often touted by fans of the squash with a pasta name. Critics may raise an eyebrow, but spaghetti squash does indeed act like spaghetti, at least as far as texture is concerned. Taste-wise, it's no surprise that the squash is more vegetal. Though it isn't soft and doughy like "real" noodles, spaghetti squash offers assorted B vitamins, vitamin K, and eye-protective antioxidants lutein and zeaxanthin, and makes a neutral, easy canvas for this cheesy dairy-free sauce.

Serves: 4–6

Ingredients:
1 medium spaghetti squash (about 6 lbs)
¾ cup raw cashews, soaked overnight
¾ cup chicken or beef broth, warmed
1 tbsp nutritional yeast
1 tbsp tamari sauce
Bragg's liquid aminos, or Coconut Secret coconut aminos
1 tsp ground turmeric
1 bunch chives, chopped, for garnish

Method:
1. Preheat oven to 400 degrees F.
2. Slice spaghetti squash lengthwise and remove seeds and pulp with a large spoon.
3. Bake until soft, about 45 minutes, in a 9" x 13" pan with one inch of water. Begin with squash face down, and turn over halfway through baking.
4. Remove from oven and cool slightly. Once cooled, use the tines of a fork to release strands into a large bowl.
5. Mix thoroughly with sauce (method below) and garnish with chopped chives.

Sauce:
1. Drain and rinse cashews and add to a blender along with all remaining ingredients.
2. Blend on high until smooth and creamy.

Let's Talk Tonics: Do You Have a Fear of Commitment?

The functional broth recipes displayed earlier are perfect for people who want to commit. Got a problem that's been bugging you? A big batch of broth will help. Got a smaller problem, or just want a quick pick-me-up? Have a tonic. These recipes are single serving cups of function, rather than potfuls. If you want them to be as potent as possible, make your tonics with the functional broth recipes that correlate.

As far as taste goes, this section is a little different. Some people balk at a mug of hot water with lemon, ginger, and cayenne for a cold; if you are one of those people, I urge you to give it a second chance. If you are a health foodie type who makes tonic beverages a part of your daily routine and can drink Chinese mushrooms teas like water, you are going to love these. If you fall somewhere in between, why not give one a try? Worst-case scenario, you will feel better than you did before and you can consider yourself a more adventurous human. All tonic recipes can be doubled or halved; recipes are mere proportions for you to reference to make any quantity you'd care to.

Ginger Love Tonic

Think of the one thing that most people really love to do, but don't always have the energy for. Yup, that's what this tonic will help you with. The ginger will increase blood flow, the fenugreek increases libido, and the ten times-concentrated maca root will help you slink right on into a loving mood, b-a-b-y. Since Longevity Power's Maca Bliss has the root's fiber removed, you need not be concerned about the common digestive upset that maca can cause.

Ingredients:
2 cups chicken or mood booster broth
2 tbsps grated fresh ginger
2 tsp Longevity Power Maca Bliss Powder
¼ tsp fenugreek powder
⅛ tsp freshly grated nutmeg to garnish

Method:
Heat all ingredients except nutmeg in a small sauce pan until very warm. Pour into mugs and garnish with freshly grated nutmeg.

Mushroom Immunity Tonic

Stave off a cold or flu on the quick with an immunity-boosting tonic full of mushroom, oregano, and silver power. They are potent ingredients that are highly effective at knocking out acute illness. The drink is small and concentrated because most people don't tend to love the taste of medicinal mushrooms; think of it more as a shooter than a sipper. *Note that modern versions of colloidal silver have been drastically reduced on the parts-per-million front. There is no risk of coloring yourself, even if you drank the whole bottle (BUT DON'T DO THAT). Sovereign Silver is known throughout the wellness industry as the most effective colloidal silver formula, and Longevity Power's Mushroom Immunity contains a blend of thirty-four different medicinal mushroom concentrates.

Serves 1

Ingredients:
¼ cup immunizer or chicken broth
½ tsp Longevity Power Mushroom Immunity Powder
3–4 drops oregano oil
1 tsp Sovereign Silver Colloidal Silver Liquid

Method:
1. Heat broth until very warm.
2. Add mushroom powder.
3. Whisk or stir until mushroom powder has dissolved, and then add oregano oil and silver.

Warming Curry Tonic

Cold weather blues never need to beat you! Heat yourself back up from within by way of curry powder with this recipe that is so simple, it scarcely even qualifies as one.

Serves 1

Ingredients:
1 cup beef or digestive broth
½ tbsp Madras curry powder

Method:
1. Heat broth in a small saucepan until very warm.
2. Add curry powder and whisk until free of lumps.

Probiotic Tonic

When my family took probiotics in the 1980s, friends and neighbors thought we were insane. It was not yet the time to discuss the "healthy bugs" living in everyone's intestines. Thankfully, that time for talking is now upon us and probiotics are becoming well known as a necessary part of life. Whether you have intestinal issues, autoimmune illness, or just want to ensure your lasting health, your belly needs lots of healthy bacteria in order for you to thrive. Combine probiotics with the gut-healing properties of bone broth and you have a recipe for happiness inside.

Serves 1

Ingredients:
½ cup digestive, immunizer or mixed poultry broth
1 tsp miso paste
½ cup liquid probiotics: unflavored kefir, unflavored kombucha, or fermented vegetable juice

Method:
1. Heat broth until just warm.
2. Remove from heat and whisk in miso paste.
3. Add liquid probiotic and stir briefly. Be sure not to add probiotics to hot liquid, as that will kill the beneficial bacteria.

Anti-inflammatory Tonic

Inflammation is often a long-term problem, but by nature it has flare-ups. During a time of discomfort, a soothing anti-inflammatory drink can bring almost immediate relief. Though bone broth contains lots of gelatin, the addition of more helps to provide extra comfort to your entire digestive system and helps your body send out fewer signals to attack.

Serves 1

Ingredients:
1 cup Inflammation Reducer, beef, or lamb broth
2 tbsps freshly grated turmeric root
1 tbsp freshly grated ginger
1 tbsp grass-fed gelatin powder

Method:

Heat all ingredients until tonic is very warm and gelatin has dissolved.

Beauty Tonic

Billy Joel and I love you just the way you are, but we—or at least I—understand completely if you have concerns about your looks. A beauty tonic is by no means as immediately effective as a cold-killing one, but over time the more foods you eat that are anti-aging, the greater the effect will be. Pearl extract has been used as a beautification tool in Chinese medicine for ages and is also a bio-available source of calcium. Beet juice fights wrinkles with folate, and the betacyanin boosts glutathione production while flushing toxins out.

Serves 1

Ingredients:
1 cup Beautifier or beef broth
2 oz. fresh beet juice
½ tsp Longevity Power Pearl Extract

Method:
Heat all ingredients until very warm, stirring to dissolve pearl powder. Do not cook beet juice, as it will be most effective raw.

Weight Loss Tonic

Though not a magic potion to make you lose half your body weight overnight, this tonic will kick-start your metabolism and curb your appetite. Lemon juice is popular for weight management because it both detoxifies you and acts as a diuretic, helping you shed excess water weight. Apple cider vinegar contains enzymes that boost your metabolism and acetic acid to regulate your blood sugar.

Serves 1

Ingredients:
1 cup Beautifier, lamb, or beef broth
Juice of 1 lemon
1 ½ tbsp raw apple cider vinegar

Method:
Heat broth in a small pot until just warmed. Remove from heat and add remaining ingredients.

Cough Remedy Tonic

I created this recipe for the most selfish of reasons: the sound of my neighbor's incessant cough was driving me nuts. One day after work I picked up a package of fresh thyme, brewed it into a super strong tea, added some broth, honey, and essential oils, and left it on her doorstep with a note that if she drank it, her cough would clear up. She stopped coughing that night, and later told me that it cured her cough completely after weeks of unsuccessfully trying "everything." I have since made it for others with nagging coughs, and so far, so cough-free for all.

Serves 1

Ingredients:
½ cup immunizer or chicken broth
½ cup thyme tea, recipe follows
2 tbsps raw honey
Optional: 2 drops each therapeutic grade peppermint, eucalyptus, and/or thyme essential oils

Method:
Thyme tea:
Brew one large handful thyme leaves in 3 cups of water for 20 minutes until liquid is reduced by half.
Tonic:
Combine all ingredients in a small pot and heat until honey is dissolved.

Allergy Tonic

If you suffer from seasonal allergies, you may use over-the-counter medications or allergy shots to get relief. While those are effective, natural remedies can work too, especially when used consistently over time, and without the side effects. Stinging nettle has been purported to relieve nearly all symptoms of seasonal allergies including runny nose, itchy and watery eyes, and sneezing. Traditional Medicinals nettle tea uses hand-harvested stinging nettles and is the best choice for those who can't find the plant locally. Local honey has long been used to strengthen one's own defenses against local allergens through the pollen it contains, and apple cider vinegar's enzymes fight infection while strengthening your immunity.

Serves 1

Ingredients:
½ cup Traditional Medicinals Nettle Tea, made per package instructions
½ cup immunizer or chicken broth
1 ½ tbsp apple cider vinegar

Method:
Heat broth in a small pot until just warm and then add remaining ingredients.

Energy Tonic

For those times when you need some pep in your step and don't want yet another cup of coffee, broth is here to your rescue. It is energizing all on its own, but by combining it with butter and Medium Chain Triglyceride oil, a concentrated form of coconut and sustainably harvested palm oils, it provides long-lasting energy that can—and should—be used as a meal replacement. The concept of adding butter and MCT oil to beverages has been popularized in recent years by "biohacker" Dave Asprey. He got the idea from sherpas who sipped yak butter tea for energy, and we have him to thank for bringing the rural tradition of drinking fats as a liquid meal replacement to the masses. The energy it provides is sustained and strong, even with liquids other than coffee. Additionally, grass-fed butter is anti-inflammatory and soothing to the digestive system, and MCT oil is antifungal, antimicrobial, antibacterial, and metabolism boosting.

Serves 1

Ingredients:
1 cup Inflammation Reducer, chicken or beef broth
1 ½ tbsp grass-fed butter (I prefer salted)
1 tbsp Bulletproof Upgraded XCT oil (read package instructions about dosage and start slowly)

Method:
1. Heat broth in a small pot until very warm.
2. Blend in a blender with remaining ingredients until smooth. Add more salt if desired.

Brocktail Recipes

This section is intentionally last, like a drink after a long workday. Obviously, the point of bone broth is not to put it with booze. It's a health food, and a powerful one at that. But what's the point of life if you can't have fun, too? Bone broth in cocktails will lighten the load on your liver a little, it provides a completely unique flavor element, and seriously, sometimes it takes alcohol to get people on board with healthful things. While I don't advocate using bone broth just for cocktails, I do see it as a nutritious addition to them and am happy to help you raise a glass with some inventive brocktail recipes.

Similar to the tonics, all recipes can be halved, doubled, or otherwise altered in quantity. Use these measurements as loose guidelines for your own creations.

After Dinner Sipper

When I was in seventh grade, my drama teacher read us "The Cask of Amontillado" by Edgar Allen Poe, and I spent days afterward saying the word "amontillado" in my head. It held such beauty for me, despite the mildly gruesome tale of Poe's about walling up an enemy that I learned it from. When I grew to drinking age, there could be only one type of sherry for me; amontillado is my favorite for reasons that have nothing at all to do with its taste, so feel free to switch it out for one you have more of an affinity for. Amontillado is a common addition for soups, so of course it pairs well with bone broth, but you could choose a drier sherry such as Fino.

Serves 1

Ingredients:
½ cup chicken broth
½ cup Amontillado sherry

Method:
Heat chicken broth in a saucepot until very warm then mix in a glass with sherry. Serve in a wine or rocks glass.

Winter Heating Pad

Serves 1

Ingredients:
¾ cup beef or lamb broth
2 oz. dark rum, spiced if preferred
1 tsp freshly grated ginger
1 drop clove therapeutic-grade essential oil

Method:
Heat beef or lamb broth in a saucepot until very warm. Remove from heat and add remaining ingredients; stir to combine. Serve in a coffee mug.

Mary Had a Little Lamb

Perhaps the most common savory cocktail in existence, adding bone broth to a Bloody Mary should be a painless step into the brocktail party. The drink by nature is salty and full of umami flavor due to Worcestershire sauce, making the addition of a dark bone broth a natural one. While Annie's organic Worcestershire does not contain the anchovies you may be used to, it also doesn't contain the "natural flavorings" and GMO sugar of regular commercial brands.

Serves 1

Ingredients:
2 oz. lamb broth
2 oz. vodka
2 oz. tomato juice
Juice of ½ lemon
2 dashes hot sauce
1 dash Annie's Naturals Organic Worcestershire Sauce
½ tsp grated horseradish root
¼ tsp celery salt
Freshly grated black pepper to taste
Garnish: celery stalk, piece of beef jerky, or pickled vegetable

Method:
1. Heat bone broth in a small pot just until room temperature and no longer gelled.
2. Combine all ingredients in a shaker with ice and shake until well combined. Serve over ice in a highball glass.

Bullshot

The Bullshot is the "original" bone broth cocktail, having been around since the 1950s. It fell by the wayside a very long time ago, but the recent reemergence of bone broth has brought it back. In short, it is a Bloody Mary that utilizes bone broth in lieu of the tomato juice, rather than in addition to as with the recipe above. To make a Bullshot, follow the recipe for Mary Had a Little Lamb, omitting tomato juice, and serve hot or over ice. The yield will be smaller, thus expressing the "shot" in the name.

Smoked Meat Supper

A cocktail of broth and an intensely smoky, delectable Scotch might not be the most nutritious dinner you have ever had, but it may not be the least, either. With just two ingredients, a smoked meat supper is a warming beverage with a campfire level of smoke yet deliciously smooth flavor.

Serves 1

Ingredients:
8 oz. chicken or mixed poultry broth
2 oz. single malt Scotch whiskey such as Ardbeg or Laphroaig

Method:
Heat broth in a small pot until very warm and add Scotch. Serve in a coffee mug.

It's About Thyme For Kale

Remember the thyme tea recipe that helps cure a cough? And remember kale, the ubiquitous green that was considered the best thing since sliced bread before bone broth usurped it? Turns out that thyme tea + booze + broth + kale = yummy stuff. It's warming, it's soothing, and it's sort of like a soup, only it can get you drunk . . . which, really, is something soups ought to learn how to do anyway.

Serves 1

Ingredients:
½ cup chicken broth
⅓ cup thyme tea, recipe follows
2 oz. cognac
2 oz. kale juice

Method:
Thyme tea:
Brew one large handful thyme leaves in 3 cups of water for 20 minutes until liquid is reduced by half.
Cocktail:
Heat broth in a small pot until very warm. Add remaining ingredients and serve in a coffee mug.

New Fashioned

The Old Fashioned is a staple for a reason: it is a simple, tasty cocktail. It went out of style for a while, but it's been back for as long as "mixology" has been a movement. I have used rye instead of bourbon to sacrifice a little sweetness, and I've left out the sugar because sweetened broth is not anyone's new, or old, friend.

Ingredients:
2 oz. rye whiskey
2 oz. beef broth
2 dashes bitters

Method:
Heat broth until room temperature and no longer gelled. Mix all ingredients in a shaker with ice and pour into a rocks glass over fresh ice.

Meatini

Call it what you will: a meat-martini, a brothtini, or a marti-brodo would all get the point across. Liven up your usual martini with broth, and make it extra dirty; olive juice and bone broth go perfectly together. If you don't have access to Square One vodka, I'd choose a non-organic top shelf brand such as Belvedere, Chopin, or Grey Goose. Lower shelf brands, even diluted with some bone broth, don't make a great martini.

Ingredients:
2 oz. Square One vodka
1 oz. chicken or beef broth
⅓ oz. olive juice

Method:
Heat broth until room temperature and no longer gelled. Mix all ingredients in a shaker with ice and pour into a martini glass.

Puesta Del Sol

Spanish for sunset, an orangey-red concoction of chipotle, carrot, mezcal, and broth will help you say goodbye to the day and hello to a relaxed evening. Of course, you could sip it through the afternoon too, because it is as full of nutritious bone broth and carrot juice as it is alcohol, and isn't life all about balance?

Ingredients:
2 oz. beef broth
2 oz. mezcal
2 oz. carrot juice
1 chipotle pepper in adobo, seeds removed, chopped finely or pureed
1 tsp adobo sauce (warning: hot!)

Method:
Heat broth in a small saucepot until room temperature and no longer gelled. Add all ingredients into a shaker with ice and shake until chilled. Serve in a high-ball glass over fresh ice.

Dr. Cucumber Pepper

A health book wouldn't be complete without at least one recipe calling for the favorite ingredient of spas the world over: cucumber. Granted, I'm not telling you to put them on your eyes or drink them at the start of your day in alkalized water (though both of those are great ideas). Instead, I have mixed cucumber with aquavit—a spirit that is similar to gin but has more herbaceous quality, chicken broth, and enough cracked black peppercorns to spice things up substantially.

Serves 1

Ingredients:
2 oz. aquavit
1 oz. chicken or mixed poultry broth
1 oz. cucumber juice
10 cracked peppercorns

Method:
Heat broth in a small saucepot until room temperature and no longer gelled. Add all ingredients into a shaker with ice and shake until chilled. Serve in a rocks glass over fresh ice.

Acknowledgments

When I began cooking, from the start I gave instructions in my head to an invisible audience. Inadvertently I set the intention to be a food writer, and twenty years later, the universe has made me one in a beautifully official way. I'd like to thank the Law of Attraction for working perfectly.

On a less ethereal level, I am deeply grateful to my management team, Sheila Conlin and Tim Ferretti of the Conlin Company, for seeing the spark in me that they have helped fan into an ever-growing fire. Sheila's dedication is ceaseless, and her guidance invaluable.

Many thanks to Holly Schmidt and Monica Sweeney of Hollan Publishing for finding bone broth and me to be a good match, and to my literary agent, Angela Rinaldi, for stepping in right on time.

I'm incredibly grateful for my private chef clients, who have helped me grow both in the kitchen and out. For my nutrition clients, I am thankful for their faith in the ability of a stranger, often over Skype, to help them get well.

Thanks to my sister, Benai, for her unique brand of loyalty, to Michelle G. for repeatedly steering me on the right path, to my mentor Arthur for seeing talent in me before I ever did, to Ace for believing in me and forcing me to cook chicken until I was comfortable with it when I was first hired by Gwyneth Paltrow, and to Pies for her love from above.

I'm blessed by the relationship with my amazing girlfriend, Michelle, who is my favorite person and my perfect fit.

Above all else, I thank my parents, Lynn and Allan Resnick. Their holistic approach to life formed the foundation of my career and allowed my creativity to bloom. They've always insisted I do the best I can, if not better than that, and they raised me with a body and soul full of love and healthy, delicious food.

References

"Aging Changes in Hair and Nails." *Medline Plus.* U.S. National Library of Medicine. 5 Nov 2012. Web. Feb 2015. http://www.nlm.nih.gov/medlineplus/ency/article/004005.htm

"Alpha-Linolenic Acid." *WebMD.* WebMD, LLC. (n.d.) Web. Feb 2015. http://www.webmd.com/vitamins-supplements/ingredientmono-1035-alpha-linolenic%20acid.aspx?activeingredientid=1035&activeingredientname=alpha-linolenic%20acid

Andrews, Sudhir. *Introduction to Tourism and Hospitality Industry.* Tata McGraw-Hill Education, 1 Jun. 2007. New Delhi. Feb 2015. https://books.google.com/books?id=PrRdc5SI_R4C&pg=PT70&lpg=PT70&dq=french+restoratif+etymology-+of+restaurant&source=bl&ots=J0-T6FLvEd&sig=XGEnd9WAKPUcX_Y-JvhxPtR-k7A&hl=en&sa=X&ei=gj3pVL7jCobGsQSDroKQDg&ved=0CDQQ6AEwBDgK#v=onepage&q=french%20restoratif%20etymology%20of%20restaurant&f=false

Ashton, Megan. "What Are the Benefits of Alpha Linolenic Acid?" *Livestrong.* Demand Media, LLC. 9 Feb. 2014. Web. Feb 2015. http://www.livestrong.com/article/388023-what-are-the-benefits-of-alpha-linolenic-acid/

"Autoimmune Disease in Women." *American Autoimmune.* American Autoimmune Related Diseases Association. (n.d.) Web. Jan. 2015. http://www.aarda.org/autoimmune-information/autoimmune-disease-in-women/

Axe, Josh Dr. "Bone Broth Benefits for Digestion, Arthritis, and Cellulite." *Dr. Axe.* (n.d.) Web. Feb. 2015. http://draxe.com/the-healing-power-of-bone-broth-for-digestion-arthritis-and-cellulite/

"Berries Gomega." *Odwalla.* Odwalla Inc. (n.d.) Web. Feb 2015. http://www.odwalla.com/products/smoothies/berries-go-mega

"Blueberry Muffin." *Dunkin Donuts.* DD IP Holder LLC. 2011. Web. Feb. 2015. http://www.dunkindonuts.com/content/dunkindonuts/en/menu/food/bakery/muffins/muffins.html?DRP_FLAVOR=Blueberry

Bibb, Emily. "The Truth Behind Your Pumpkin Spice Latte." *Popsugar.* Popsugar.com 13 Sept. 2014. Web. Feb 2015. http://www.popsugar.com/fitness/Starbucks-Pumpkin-Spice-Latte-763582

"Bone Broth." *Hemsley Hemsley.* Hemsley + Hemsley LTD. (n.d.) Web. Jan. 2015. http://www.hemsleyandhemsley.com/recipe/bone-broth/

Busch, Sandi. "Alpha-Lipoic Acid vs. Conjugated Linoleic Acid." *Livestrong.* Demand Media, Inc. 21 May 2014. http://www.livestrong.com/article/475972-alpha-lipoic-acid-vs-conjugated-linoleic-acid/

Butler, Stephanie. "More Than Chicken Soup: Food Remedies." *Hungry History.* A&E Television Networks, LLC. 28 Sept. 2012. Web. Jan. 2015. http://www.history.com/news/hungry-history/more-than-chicken-soup-food-remedies

"Calcium: Dietary Supplement Fact Sheet." *Office of Dietary Supplements.* National Institute of Health. 21 Nov. 2013. Web. Jan. 2015 http://ods.od.nih.gov/factsheets/Calcium-HealthProfessional/

"Calcium: National Nutrient Database for Standard Reference." *United States Department of Agricultural Research Service.* The National Agricultural Library. (n.d.) Web. Feb. 2015. http://ndb.nal.usda.gov/ndb/nutrients/report?nutrient1=301&nutrient2=&nutrient3=&fg=&max=25&subset=0&offset=75&sort=c&totCount=8037&measureby=m

"Chicken Soup." *Drugs.com* (n.d.) Web. Jan. 2015. http://www.drugs.com/npp/chicken-soup.html

"Chicken Soup." *Wikipedia, The Free Encyclopedia.* Wikimedia Foundation, Inc. 21 Jan. 2015. Web. Jan. 2015. http://en.wikipedia.org/wiki/Chicken_soup

Coleman, Erin R.D., L.D. "Bone Broth Nutrition Facts." *Livestrong.* Demand Media, Inc. 6 Feb 2014. Web. Jan 2015. http://www.livestrong.com/article/369817-beef-broth-nutrition-facts/

Coman, Julia. "Origins of 'First' Restaurant Challenged After 200 Years." *The Telegraph.* Telegraph Media Group Limited. 3 Sept. 2000. Web. Feb 2015. http://www.telegraph.co.uk/news/worldnews/1353970/Origins-of-first-restaurant-challenged-after-200-years.html

Crooks, Ross. "Splurge Vs. Save: Which Beauty Products are Worth the Extra Cost?" *Mintlife.* Intuit, Inc. 11 April 2013. Web. Feb 2015.

https://www.mint.com/blog/consumer-iq/splurge-vs-save-which-beauty-products-are-worth-the-extra-cost-0413/

"Early Pottery at 20,000 Years Ago in Xianrendong Cave, China." *Science*. American Association for the Advancement of Science. Vol. 336 no 6089 pp1696-1700. 29 June 2012. Web. Feb 2015. http://www.sciencemag.org/content/336/6089/1696

Elkaim, Yuri. "Leaky Gut: What It Is and How to Heal It." *U.S. News Health*. U.S. News and World Report LP. 6 Mar. 2014. Web. Feb. 2015. http://health.usnews.com/health-news/blogs/eat-run/2014/03/06/leaky-gut-what-it-is-and-how-to-heal-it

Ellin, Abby. "Beauty Spots." *New York Times*. The New York Times Company. 3 April 2011. Web. Feb 2015. http://www.nytimes.com/2013/04/04/fashion/hair-products-with-collagen-beauty-spots.html

"Free Glutamic Acid (MSG): Sources and Dangers." *Nutrition Digest*. American Nutrition Association. Volume 37, No. 2. (n.d.) Web. Feb. 2015. http://americannutritionassociation.org/newsletter/free-glutamic-acid-msg-sources-dangers

Galarza, Daniela. "The Bone Broth Trend Isn't Going Anywhere: Here's What You Need to Know." *Eater*. Vox Media. 12 Feb. 2015. Web. Feb. 2015. http://www.eater.com/2015/2/12/8025027/what-is-bone-broth-and-why-is-everyone-talking-about-it

Gibbons, Jacqui. "Bone Broth: Should You Eat it and How Did It Become the First Health Food Trend of 2015?" *High 50 Health*. High 50 LTD. 26 Jan. 2015. Web. Feb 2015. http://www.high50.com/us/health/bone-broth-should-you-eat-it-and-how-did-it-become-the-first-health-food-trend-of-2015

Goldman, Erik. "A New Approach to Promoting Healthy Sleep." *Holistic Primary Care*. Holistic Primary Care. 8 Dec. 2011. Web. Jan 2015. http://www.holisticprimarycare.net/topics/topics-o-z/vitamins-a-supplements/1249-a-new-approach-to-promoting-healthy-sleep-

Golembewski, Vanessa. "In Defense of Being High Maintenance." *Refinery 29*. Refinery 29. 6 Aug. 2013. Web. Feb 2015. http://www.refinery29.com/2013/08/50961/high-maintenance#page-3

"Grass Fed Meat and Dairy" *Food Graphs*. Societas, Inc. 2009. Web. Feb 2015.
http://www.foodgraphs.net/food/grassfed.html

"Grass Fed Beef for Omega-3s?" *Berkeley Wellness*. Remedy Health Media, LLC. 7 Jan.
2015. Web. Feb 2015.
http://www.berkeleywellness.com/healthy-eating/food/nutrition/article/grass-fed-
beef-omega-3s

Hajoway, Mike. "Conjugated Linoleic Acid." *Body Building*. BodyBuilding.com LLC. 2
Jun. 2014. Web. Jan. 2015.
http://www.bodybuilding.com/fun/mike8.htm

Holmes, Baxter. "Chicken Soup for the Aging Star's Soul." *ESPN*. ESPN Internet Ventures. 15 Jan. 2015. Web. Jan. 2015.
http://espn.go.com/nba/story/_/id/12168515/bone-broth-soup-helping-los-angeles-
lakers-kobe-bryant

"Inflammation." *Arizona Center for Advanced Medicine*. (n.d.) Web. Jan. 2015.
http://www.arizonaadvancedmedicine.com/articles/inflammation.html

Ipatenco, Sara. "The SIBO Diet." *Livestrong*. Demand Media, Inc. 20 May 2014. Web.
Feb 2015.
http://www.livestrong.com/article/318789-the-sibo-diet/

Wolf, Nicki. "Chicken Broth Nutrition." *Livestrong*. Deman Media, Inc. 18 Feb. 2015.
Web. Feb 2015.
http://www.livestrong.com/article/368293-chicken-broth-nutrition/

"Irritable Bowel Syndrome." *WebMD*. WebMD UK Limited. (n.d.) Web. Feb 2015.
http://www.webmd.boots.com/ibs/guide/irritable-bowel-syndrome

"Irritable Bowel Syndrome." *Wikipedia, The Free Encyclopedia*. Wikimedia Foundation,
Inc. 21 Jan. 2015. Web. Jan. 2015.
http://en.wikipedia.org/wiki/Irritable_bowel_syndrome

Koenig, Laura. "Chicken Soup Around the World." *My Jewish Learning*. 70/Faces Media.
(n.d.) Web. Feb 2015.
http://www.myjewishlearning.com/culture/2/Food/Ashkenazic_Cuisine/Poland_and_
Russia/chickensoup.shtml

Loe, Theresa. "Decoding the Terms: Cage Free, Free Range, & Pasture-Raised Eggs."
Living Homegrown. Living Homegrown. (n.d.) Web. Feb 2015.

http://www.livinghomegrown.com/decoding-the-terms-cage-free-free-range-pasture-raised-eggs/

"Magnesium: Fact Sheet for Health Professionals." *Office of Dietary Supplements.* National Institute of Health. 4 Nov. 2013. Web. Jan. 2015 http://ods.od.nih.gov/factsheets/Magnesium-HealthProfessional/

Mayo Clinic Staff. "High Blood Pressure (Hypertension)." *Mayo Clinic.* Mayo Foundation for Medical Education and Research. (n.d.) Web. Feb 2015. http://www.mayoclinic.org/diseases-conditions/high-blood-pressure/basics/definition/con-20019580

Mayo Clinic Staff. "How to Tame Your Salt Habit." *Mayo Clinic.* Mayo Foundation for Medical Education and Research. (n.d.) Web. Feb 2015. http://www.mayoclinic.org/healthy-living/nutrition-and-healthy-eating/in-depth/sodium/art-20045479

Morell, Sally Fallon; Daniel, Kayla T. PhD, CCN. *Nourishing Broth: An Old-Fashioned Remedy for the Modern World.* Grand Central Life & Style. Boston. 2014. (Jan. 2015.)

Moskin, Julia. "Bones, Broth, Bliss." *New York Times.* The New York Times Company. 6 Jan. 2015. Web. Jan. 2015. http://www.nytimes.com/2015/01/07/dining/bone-broth-evolves-from-prehistoric-food-to-paleo-drink.html?_r=0

Mueller, Christina. "Do Collagen Supplements Actually Get Rid of Wrinkles?" *Prevention.* Prevention Magazine. 15 July 2014. Web. Feb 2015. http://www.prevention.com/beauty/skin-care/do-collagen-supplements-work-any-better-wrinkle-creams

Mychaskiw, Marianne. "Report: Women Spend an Average of $15,000 on Makeup in Their Lifetime." *InStyle.* Time, Inc. Style Network. 17 April 2014. Web. Feb. 2015. http://news.instyle.com/2013/04/17/women-makeup-spending-facts/

Myers, Amy. "9 Signs You Have Leaky Gut." *Mind Body Green.* Mind Body Green LLC. 12 Sept. 2013. Web. Feb 2015. http://www.mindbodygreen.com/0-10908/9-signs-you-have-a-leaky-gut.html

Oliver, Dana. "What Hair Dye is Really Doing to Your Hair." *The Huffington Post.* TheHuffingtonPost.com Inc. 1 Nov. 2013. Web. Jan. 2015. http://www.huffingtonpost.com/2013/11/01/hair-dye-process_n_4181186.html

Olver, Lynn. "Food Timeline." *Food Timeline Library*. Lynne Olver. 2 Jan. 2015. Web. Feb 2015.
http://www.foodtimeline.org/foodsoups.html

"Phosphorous In Diet." *Medline Plus*. U.S. National Library of Medicine. 18 Feb 2013. Web. Feb 2015.
http://www.nlm.nih.gov/medlineplus/ency/article/002424.htm

"Phosphorous: National Nutrient Database for Standard Reference." *United States Department of Agricultural Research Service*. The National Agricultural Library. (n.d.) Web. Feb. 2015.
http://ndb.nal.usda.gov/ndb/nutrients/report?nutrient1=305&nutrient2=&nutrient3=&fg=&max=25&subset=0&offset=7200&sort=c&totCount=7818&measureby=m

"Potassium." *Wikipedia, The Free Encyclopedia*. Wikimedia Foundation, Inc. 21 Jan. 2015. Web. Jan. 2015.
http://en.wikipedia.org/wiki/Potassium

Rennard, Barbara O. et al. "Chicken Soup Inhibits Neutrophil Chemotaxis In Vitro." *Chest Journal*. Vol 118, No 4. American College of Chest Physicians. Oct. 2000. Web. Feb. 2015.
http://journal.publications.chestnet.org/article.aspx?articleid=1079188

Repinski, Karyn. "Face Facts: Too Much Sugar Can Cause Wrinkles." *NBC News*. NBCNews.com 21 Oct. 2007. Web. Feb 2015.
http://www.nbcnews.com/id/21257751/ns/health-skin_and_beauty/t/face-facts-too-much-sugar-can-cause-wrinkles/#.VMqCIWTF--W

Saint Louise, Catherine. "Up the Career Ladder, Lipstick in Hand." *New York Times*. The New York Times Company. 12 Oct. 2011. Web. Feb 2015. http://www.nytimes.com/2011/10/13/fashion/makeup-makes-women-appear-more-competent-study.html?_r=1&

Sarah. "Gelatin and Collagen Hydrosylate: What's the Difference?" *The Healthy Home Economist*. Austus Foods LLC. (n.d) Web. Feb 2015.
http://www.thehealthyhomeeconomist.com/gelatin-and-collagen-hydrolysate-whats-the-difference/

Weeks, Caitlin. "The Top 20 Health Benefits of Gelatin." *Grass Fed Girl*. Grass Fed Girl LLC. 15 Feb. 2014. Web. Feb 2015.

http://www.grassfedgirl.com/top-20-health-benefits-of-gelatin-helps-prevent-arthritis-cellulite-stretch-marks-wrinkles-brittle-bones-and-more/

Weisul, Kimberly. "This Entrepreneur Wants to Make Bone Broth the Next Juice." *Inc.* Inc.com 27 Jan. 2015. Web. Jan 2015.
http://www.inc.com/kimberly-weisul/the-entrepreneur-behind-new-yorks-latest-food-craze.htm

Woodard, Stephanie. "6 Natural Remedies that Really Work." *NBC News.* NBCNews.com 19 Mar. 2010.
http://www.nbcnews.com/id/35063075/ns/health-alternative_medicine/t/natural-remedies-really-work/#.VOk3QrDF--Ui

"Understanding Autoinflammatory Diseases." *NIH.* National Institutes of Health. March 2010. Web. Feb 2015.
http://www.niams.nih.gov/health_info/autoinflammatory/

"What is SIBO?" *WebMD.* WebMD UK Limited. (n.d.) Web. Feb 2015.
http://www.webmd.boots.com/digestive-disorders/small-intestinal-bacteria-sibo?page=2

"Why Is Potassium Important?" *WebMD.* WebMD, LLC. (n.d.) Web. Feb 2015.
http://www.webmd.com/a-to-z-guides/potassium-content-of-fruits-vegetables-and-other-foods-topic-overview

Yu, Su-Mei. "Su-Mei Yu's Long Life Chicken Broth." *Good Morning America.* ABC News Internet Ventures. (n.d.) Web. Feb. 2015.
http://abcnews.go.com/GMA/recipe?id=8879350

Zeilinksi, Sarah. "Stone Age Stew? Soup Making May Be Older Than We'd Thought." *NPR.* NPR. 6 Nov. 2013. Web. Feb 2015.
http://www.npr.org/blogs/thesalt/2013/02/06/171104410/stone-age-stew-soup-making-may-be-older-than-wed-thought

Zeratsky, Katherine R.D., L.D. "What is MSG? Is it Bad For You?" *Mayo Clinic.* Mayo Foundation for Medical Education and Research. (n.d) Web. Feb 2015.
http://www.mayoclinic.org/healthy-living/nutrition-and-healthy-eating/expert-answers/monosodium-glutamate/faq-20058196